# EVERY STONE
# A STORY
## MANITOBA'S
## BURIED HISTORY

**CHARLES BRAWN AND DALE BRAWN**

GREAT PLAINS
PUBLICATIONS

Great Plains Publications
420 – 70 Arthur Street
Winnipeg, MB  R3B 1G7
www.greatplains.mb.ca

Great Plains Publications gratefully acknowledges the financial support provided for its publishing program by the Government of Canada through the Book Publishing Industry Development Program (BPIDP); the Canada Council for the Arts; as well as the Manitoba Department of Culture, Heritage and Tourism; and the Manitoba Arts Council.

Design & Typography by Relish Design Studio Ltd.
Printed in Canada by Friesens

**Library and Archives Canada Cataloguing in Publication**

Brawn, Charles, 1923-
    Every stone a story : Manitoba's buried history, 1900-2000 / Charles Brawn and Dale Brawn.


ISBN 978-1-894283-79-3


    1. Manitoba–Biography. 2. Sepulchral monuments–Manitoba.
3. Manitoba–History–20th century. I. Brawn, Dale, 1948- II. Title.

FC3355.B73 2008          971.27009'9          C2008-901687-4

*To Doreen Lois Brawn, our most enthusiastic*
*and devoted supporter*

*and to Findlay Paterson Bergstra (1983-2006)*
*a much missed friend*

# CONTENTS

PREFACE

# preface

Every father-son relationship is different. While all are multi-layered, the best are grounded in a shared enthusiasm. Ours is for cemeteries.

This book describes the lives of some of the famous, infamous and even unknown women and men who have lived in Manitoba. Some stories have been told before, like those of politicians Thomas Mayne Daly and Sir Clifford Sifton, author Philip Grove, embezzler John Machray, scientist Louis Slotin, serial killer Earle 'the Strangler' Nelson and pioneer Squire Sowden. Their stories, in our opinion, deserve re-telling.

The lives and deaths of many of the people described in this book, however, have never previously been told. Paul Wolos, for instance, was a high school student who died on a battlefield in Vietnam; and Lawrence Lees, a dedicated game warden, murdered because he did his job too well.

Many of the people we wrote about faced death with incredible bravery. As Stanley McInnis slowly lost his life to the poison which spread from his ruptured appendix, for example, he shared his dying as he had done his life, surrounded by those who wanted nothing more than to bask in his friendship; and Brandon's first police chief clung tenaciously to life after mortally wounding himself until he could say a last goodbye to his wife.

Occasionally the stories we describe are, to put it mildly, unusual. In one case the body of a Titanic victim arrived minutes before his funeral, only it turned out not to be his body. Another life story is that of a wife-killer whose last request was to be buried beside his victim. He was, but not for long. His wife's distraught family quickly moved her remains far from those of the man who took her life.

In our many visits to the cemeteries and archives of Manitoba we met dozens of people who did much to make this book a reality. Among that number are Tom Mitchell, DeLloyd Guth, Eileen Trott, Sandy Jasper, Norm Reid, Jill Hannah-Kayes, Bill Fardoe, Lyle Gawletz, Isabel Ferguson, Lloyd Franklin, Dorothy Beswitherick, Helen Aylwin, Milly and Steve Mycashiw, Marion Kotulsky and Stella Handzuk.

We would especially like to acknowledge Ewan Pow and Grant Hamilton of the *Brandon Sun*, and Angela and Gary Brawn, whose help, encouragement and advice have been invaluable.

—*Charles and Dale Brawn*

LIKE SO MANY PRAIRIE PIONEERS, the people described in this chapter are remembered not because of a single act, but because of a life dedicated to others. Some, like Squire Sowden, founded a town. Charles Boulton too was a community leader, but he was also an adventurer whose life was entwined with that of Louis Riel, the father of Manitoba. Abraham Klenman, like Adam McKenzie, was equal measures farmer and immigration promoter. Chief One Arrow, on the other hand, not only did not promote settlement of the prairies, he became a victim of it. The lives of the two men who typified the dedication of rural doctors everywhere are important to remember because they illustrate how so few accomplished so much for so many. Eleanor Cripss, like Boulton, was both an adventurer and a person truly of her time. That was even more the case for Charles Sankey, one of the last of the swashbucklers of the high seas.

# CHAPTER 1

# pioneers

# 1823-1907

# WILLIAM HENRY "SQUIRE" SOWDEN

Cantankerous, ambitious, imaginative and visionary were just a few of the words used by contemporaries to describe the man who founded the town of Souris. History, however, remembers him for his opera house, palatial home, and of course, his swinging bridge.

William Henry Squire Sowden was born in Port Hope, Upper Canada, in 1823. He married Mary Ann Ashford twenty-eight years later, and the two were the parents of one child, William Frederick Sowden. All three were to play a significant role in the settlement of the Glenwood district southwest of Brandon.

In 1872 Ottawa passed an act allowing anyone who was at least twenty one years old to apply for a homestead right to 160 acres of unsettled land in the west. Title would be granted to homesteaders after three years if they had resided on the property they claimed and had made the required improvements. Homesteaders were also given a pre-emption privilege that allowed them to buy an adjoining quarter section of land for one dollar per acre.

In July 1880 a group of businessmen from Millbrook, Ontario, decided to take advantage of the government's offer to grant colonization companies the right to purchase large sections of the prairie west if they agreed to attract settlers to the region. The Millbrook group, consisting of Sowden, John Nesbit Kirchhoffer, Major S. G. Fairblough and a number of other venture capitalists, formed the Millbrook Manitoba Land Company and the Sowden Colonization Company. In the fall of that year Sowden was sent on a scouting expedition that took him as far west as Saskatchewan. In the end, however, he selected the Souris district for the group's project.

After their proposal was accepted by Ottawa the Millbrook organizers began advertising for settlers. Those who signed up in Ontario were to have first choice of homesteads and pre-emptions. Most paid $3.00 per acre for their land, fifty cents more than the price paid by Sowden. In addition, emigrants received a preferential rate for their railway transportation to Manitoba.

The Sowden party left Millbrook on the evening of April 5th, 1881, and travelled west via Detroit, Chicago and St. Paul, Minnesota. They arrived in St. Boniface about three o'clock in the afternoon exactly one week later. A letter written by one of the party gave a first hand impression of what they found. "Everyone I meet here says that the Souris district is the best up here, and that we will be delighted with it. There are hundreds going west each day, and it is almost impossible to get cars to Portage, there are so many waiting to go."

The first of the Sowden settlers arrived at Plum Creek on April 27th and the remainder the following day. Choosing homesteads, however, did not go as planned. Groups of pioneers who knew nothing of the arrangements Ottawa had made with Sowden had arrived in the area earlier in the spring, and some ended up with land that should rightly have gone to others.

The new settlers wasted little time in settling in. They held their first church service on Sunday, May 8th, and ten days later met to form an agricultural society. A third meeting was held on May 24 to discuss construction of a bridge across the Souris River and to establish a post office.

Construction started immediately. The first building in the new town was a log blacksmith shop on the bank of Plum Creek, and the first residence a substantial log house built by Sowden on the east side of the waterway.

By 1904 Sowden was the owner of a number of lots in a subdivision which he hoped would become the town's first suburb. Most of the community lay on the west bank of the river, however, and Sowden became convinced that to sell his lots he would have to provide a direct route to the downtown business district.

He solved the problem by building a foot bridge across the creek. The structure was three feet wide and 582 feet long, and consisted of boards nailed to four-by-fours, supported by two wire cables. Page wire ran along each side to prevent pedestrians from falling into the creek.

Within a month, however, a strong wind tossed the bridge around so violently that it eventually flipped over. Undaunted, Sowden simply added more stability by attaching guide wires to either side of the platform. When he gave the bridge to the town a few years later even more

When he gave the bridge to the town a few years later even more stability was added by anchoring cables to cement blocks buried on each river bank.

stability was added by anchoring cables to cement blocks buried on each river bank.

Sowden's creation is now one of the most famous swinging bridges in North America, and the longest in Canada. The 177-metre walkway was destroyed by a flood in 1976 and rebuilt the following year. In April 2005 it was featured on a postage stamp sold across Canada.

Squire Sowden died on April 26, 1907 and is buried in the Souris cemetery beside other members of his family. ✦

# 1841-1899

# CHARLES ARKOLL BOULTON

Charles Arkoll Boulton was born in April 1841 into a family with strong connections to the military and political élites of Upper Canada. After graduating from the prestigious Upper Canada College he entered the military and served at Gibraltar, Malta and Montreal. In 1868 he sold his commission and the following year joined the survey party sent to the Red River Settlement in anticipation of a rush of settlers to the region after its annexation to Canada.

When the Métis under Louis Riel resisted the imposition of Canadian rule and established a provisional government, Boulton was asked to organize volunteers to help put down the uprising. He was a weak and ineffectual leader, however, and the Métis had no difficulty taking him prisoner. Acutely aware of the seriousness of the threat posed by the group, Riel demanded that an example be made of Boulton. He was tried and sentenced to death for interference with the provisional government. Intercessions on his behalf resulted in his pardon, and Boulton was released to return to Ontario, where he operated a sawmill until collapsing markets for sawn lumber forced him into bankruptcy.

• Charles Arkoll
Boulton

Boulton returned to the prairies in 1880 to establish a homestead in the Shell River valley. He was in Winnipeg in late March 1885, however, when news of rebellion in the North-West Territories arrived. He immediately offered his services to the commander of the Canadian militia. Granted a commission, Boulton returned home to raise two troops of volunteers, one from Russell and the other from Birtle. The unit's final complement included five officers and 123 soldiers. Boulton's Scouts joined the main Canadian force as it advanced towards Fish Creek and Batoche, and it became the only Manitoba company to play a major role in the subsequent fighting. Boulton's hatred of his former nemesis was so well known that, when Riel agreed to surrender, Boulton and his men were sent out on a wild-goose chase to ensure that they did not harm the Métis leader.

Boulton's unit was disbanded in September 1885. When the 32nd Manitoba Horse was formed a quarter century later it considered Boulton's Scouts to be its ancestor.

Almost immediately after returning home Boulton published *Reminiscences of the North-West Rebellions,* an account of his involvement in the Riel uprising, and began lobbying the federal government for a patronage appointment. He also farmed, maintained a general store and participated in the formation of the Manitoba Dairy Association. In 1887 Boulton ran in the federal election in the federal constituency of Marquette, losing by 58 votes. Two years later he finally secured his reward and was appointed to the Canadian Senate.

Boulton's career and financial difficulties were similar to those of thousands of 19th century Manitoba settlers, who also saw their dreams of prosperity evaporate in the reality of western pioneering. Boulton died of pneumonia on 15 May 1899 and is buried in the Russell cemetery. ✦

# 1825-1910

## ABRAHAM KLENMAN

**A**braham Klenman was born on the border of Romania and Russia in 1825. The story of the struggle he went through to honour the traditions of his people, while at the same time making a home for his family in a strange new land, is a revealing tale of what members of religious minorities went through when they arrived in Canada's unsettled west.

For Jews born in Russia the 19th century was a time of tremendous hardship. For centuries the government had imposed a myriad number of legal restrictions on its Jewish citizens, including limiting their ability to travel, abolishing their right to settle on and own land, forcing them into years of military servitude, and imposing quotas for their admission to high schools and universities. When Czar Alexander II was assassinated in 1881 conditions became even worse, as a wave of government-sanctioned assaults on Jews, known as pogroms, spread across the nation, leaving thousands either dead or homeless.

As a result of these attacks there was a huge exodus of Jews from all over the country, but particularly of those living in Bessarabia and Southern Russia. Coincidental with their emigration were the first attempts by the government of Canada to attract Europeans to

> Unlike other groups, who were encouraged to settle blocks of land, the Canadian government forced Jews to take homesteads among their non-Jewish neighbours.

its vast undeveloped west. The propaganda which reached prospective immigrants was persuasive, especially since it omitted any reference to the primitive conditions of the prairies. These included long and severe winters, a short growing season, and things like frost, hail, drought, rust and grasshoppers.

Although every pioneer faced the same physical hardships, for prospective Jewish farmers conditions in western Canada were especially difficult. Most arrived with virtually no farming experience, and the occupations into which had been forced, like that of small shopkeeper and petty tradesman, did little to prepare them for the vagaries of the Canadian frontier.

Notwithstanding their lack of experience, however, Jews were among the first Europeans to establish agricultural settlements in the west. Among their number Klenman was

particularly unique, in that he actually had farming experience, having worked rented land as a young man. Although barred from owning property in the land of his birth, he nonetheless believed that a return to the land was necessary for Jews to fulfill their destiny.

When Klenman arrived in Montreal in 1888 he immediately began advocating establishment of a Jewish agricultural colony on the prairies, and a few months later he and another Jewish immigrant headed west to find suitable land. In Winnipeg they sought out the assistance of the land commissioner of the Canadian Pacific Railway Company, and on his advice traveled throughout the northwest. Eventually they decided on land near Wapella, a small Saskatchewan community twenty miles from the Manitoba border and near New Jerusalem, which four years earlier had become the nation's first Jewish farming community.

Unlike other groups, who were encouraged to settle blocs of land, the Canadian government forced Jews to take homesteads among their non-Jewish neighbours. This was troubling to Jewish settlers, who needed to be near other Jews not only for mutual assistance and protection but for religious reasons.

The Russian Jews who helped settle the west were orthodox, and prayer services were an integral part of their daily lives. To conduct such services Jewish tradition required a *minyan,* or group of at least ten adult males. In the late nineteenth century transportation problems, which made it difficult to travel to and from isolated farms, meant that a settlement in which homesteads were located even a few miles apart was unacceptable to the devotedly religious. As a consequence, the Department of the Interior and the CPR eventually agreed to interchange land each owned, so that Klenman and members of his settlement group could obtain adjacent homesteads.

Within a decade of his arrival in the Wapella area fifty Jewish families had joined Klenman. Most became mixed farmers, although some supplemented incomes by cutting firewood and selling it in adjacent villages. All, however, were possessed of a strong will to succeed. Wapella not only became the longest-surviving Jewish farm colony in the country, it served as the model and training ground for other Jewish agricultural settlements.

When Klenman died in 1910 Jewish tradition required that he be buried as soon as possible. In small communities this usually meant by sundown of the day of a person's death. Klenman, however, had insisted that his body be transported to Brandon, where his son had moved some years earlier, for interment in that city's Jewish cemetery.

When his remains arrived in Brandon a *chevra kadisha,* or Jewish "burial society," immediately took control of them. Then, as now, its job was to insure that the bodies of Jews were prepared for burial according to Jewish law. At

Once Klenman's body was cleansed it was dressed in a shroud made of ten pieces of pure white cotton, and his plain wooden casket was sealed, since in Jewish tradition it was considered disrespectful to stare at someone who cannot look back.

the heart of the society's function was the ritual of purification, in which a body was thoroughly cleansed and then ritually purified by immersion in, or under, a continuous flow of water. Once Klenman's body was cleansed it was dressed in a shroud made of ten pieces of pure white cotton, and his plain wooden casket was sealed, since in Jewish tradition it was considered disrespectful to stare at someone who cannot look back.

Abraham Klenman was eighty-five years old when he died. He is buried beside his wife Pearl and son Alexander in Brandon's B'nai Israel cemetery. ✦

# 1848-1926

## ADAM "THE FABULOUS SCOT" MCKENZIE

In the history of Canada few have played a more important role in the settlement of Manitoba than the 'fabulous Scot.' He was among the first to open for cultivation the plains between Portage la Prairie and Carberry, generating success for an entire generation of farmers.

Adam McKenzie was born on 22 March 1848 near what is now Guelph, Ontario. Two years before Manitoba entered Confederation (1870) he and his family settled just west of Portage. Neither the McKenzies nor the handful of other settlers arriving in the province were welcomed by those already living there. Cultivating land hurt the business of local trappers and fur traders, and it infuriated Aboriginals, who often stole the livestock and supplies of settlers in an attempt to drive them from the area. Such activities, however, did not deter the McKenzies.

Soon the federal government launched an aggressive campaign to encourage more agricultural settlement on the prairies. Legislation entitled a settler to 160 acres of land for only $10.00 if the homesteader resided on the claim for six months, built a permanent residence, and broke at least forty acres within three years. If these conditions were satisfied the settler could purchase, or pre-empt, an adjacent quarter section of land for about $2.00 an acre.

In 1872 Adam McKenzie left his father's homestead to follow the Saskatchewan Trail beyond Manitoba's western boundary, into a part of the North-West Territories soon known as Beautiful Plains. He and his wife Catherine McEachern spent their first winter near Arden in a crude log building which doubled as a government office and a supply base for surveyors.

The following spring the McKenzies moved to their homestead and constructed a house of their own. Typically such a home was made of logs trimmed with a broad-axe, hoisted into position before the corners dove-tailed. Although nothing is known of the McKenzie's roof, most were either sod or thatch-grass.

McKenzie was an exceptionally hard-working farmer, and easily the largest landholder in the area. According to Grant MacEwan, in the 1870s a settler could claim all the land he could plough in one day with a yoke of oxen. McKenzie is credited with ploughing "the longest furrow ever cut on the earth's crust."

In 1876 the Scotsman took what grain he had on hand and arranged to have it ground into flour at Gladstone. He then loaded each of thirty-two carts with twenty sacks of flour and headed west to Edmonton. The carts were built entirely of wood and his wagon train was accompanied by a herd of replacement animals under the supervision of three or four Métis.

In Edmonton McKenzie sold his load for $20 a sack, together with his oxen, and returned home to purchase more land on the Carberry plains. He employed a number of farm hands, using an ingenious device neighbours referred to as a 'gatling gun' that sowed more than one hundred acres a day. Over the next twenty years McKenzie purchased almost 14,000 acres, mainly to be rented out.

He was an astute businessman, earning a considerable income from the oxen, horses, hogs and seed grain he sold to newcomers. He was not, however, greedy. When the rate of interest charged on loans was eight per cent he charged six, and if a loan was paid on time, he took no interest at all.

Years of hard work eventually took its toll and he sold his holdings and retired to British Columbia. He was soon bored, though, and returned to Manitoba. When he heard good things about Cuba, he again left for greener pastures. His stay in the Caribbean was short, however, and this time he returned both wiser and poorer for his experience.

Adam McKenzie died on 25 October 1926 and is buried beside his wife in the Burnside Cemetery just west of Portage la Prairie. ✦

# 1886

## CHIEF ONE ARROW

**CHIEF ONE ARROW**
Signatory to treaty #6
KA – PAYAK – WASKUNAM
1830 – 1886

CHIEF ONE ARROW, chief of a Willow
Cree Tribe along the Saskatchewan River,
was incarcerated at Stony Mountain for
his participation in the North – West
Rebellion of 1885. He was released and
died shortly thereafter in Arch – Bishop
Lachu's residency, St. Boniface, Manitoba.
Apr. 25, 1886

His last words to the Government
of Canada were:
"Do not mistreat my people."

O ne of the abiding injustices of Canadian history is the way the government of this country's first prime minister treated the natives of western Canada in the years leading up to, and following, the Riel Rebellion of 1885. And no one was more poorly treated than One Arrow, the chief of a band of Willow Crees.

When Canada became a nation in 1867 the Crees still ranged from the Rocky Mountains of western North America to the Atlantic seaboard of the continent's east coast. Until the disappearance of the buffalo from the Canadian prairies ten years later, members of One Arrow's tribe hunted in a region bisected by the South Saskatchewan River, stretching from near Duck Lake in the north to Little Manitou Lake and Goose Lake to the south. By 1879, however, starving and decimated by smallpox, the band settled permanently on a sixteen square-mile reserve four miles east of the South Saskatchewan River, behind the Métis settlement of Batoche, Saskatchewan.

When Louis Riel returned to Canada from exile in Montana in 1884, to once again negotiate with the federal government on behalf of a group of disaffected Métis, he quickly realized that his followers were not the only people living in the west who had become disillusioned with the way they were being treated by Ottawa. One

Arrow's band was one of several which had not received from the government the implements and livestock promised in 1876 under the terms of Treaty No. 6.

Although the Cree chieftain did not come into national prominence until after the outbreak of the rebellion, in 1880 he had been arrested on a charge of inciting his followers to butcher government cattle as an act of protest. A jury refused to convict him, however. Four years later One Arrow attended a large council of chiefs to discuss Indian grievances, and despite playing only a minor role in the proceedings, he succeeded in attracting the attention of the government.

Since his reserve was closest to the Métis settlement on the South Saskatchewan River, One Arrow's followers were the most susceptible to Métis influence. Still, in mid-March 1885 a federal Indian agent was able to obtain a profession of loyalty from the chief. The fate of the Cree leader was sealed, however, when the agent was taken prisoner by Louis Riel and about forty Métis as he left the reserve. Although One Arrow and his band played no part in the capture, the following day they were seen butchering the reserve's cattle and became the first band openly to join the rebels. The chief and his men were subsequently seen armed and in the company of Riel and his Métis, both following the battle at Duck Lake and around the Métis settlement of Batoche.

When the rebellion was finally put down One Arrow was arrested on a charge of treason-felony and tried at Regina. There appeared to have been some legitimacy to his argument that he was too old and feeble to have taken an active part in the hostilities. In 1882, for example, he attempted to resign his chieftainship on grounds of his advanced old age and poor health. During his trial One Arrow appeared confused, and the only witness called to testify on his behalf failed to appear. To make matters worse, the prosecution's evidence was poorly translated into Cree. When the charges were explained to him, One Arrow was told that he was being charged with 'knocking off the Queen's bonnet and stabbing her in the behind with a sword.' The confused chief was so puzzled by the claim that he accused his interpreter of being drunk.

Although One Arrow did not speak during the trial, after his conviction he denied actively participating in the rebellion and suggested that whatever he had done was the result of pressure by Riel and Gabriel Dumont. His protestations, however, fell on deaf ears. He and Poundmaker and Big Bear were each sentenced to three years in Stony Mountain Penitentiary.

In prison One Arrow's health quickly deteriorated, and after serving only seven months of his sentence he was released. During his brief incarceration he converted to Roman Catholicism and, on his release, unable to walk, he was carried to the residence of the archbishop of St Boniface, Alexandre-Antonin Taché. For the next two weeks the once proud chief lingered between life and death. On Easter Sunday, 25 April 1886, he died.

His headstone bears the inscription:

*Chief One Arrow, chief of a Willow Cree Tribe along the Saskatchewan River, was incarcerated at Stony Mountain for his participation in the North-West Rebellion of 1885. He was released and died shortly thereafter in Archbishop Taché's residence, St. Boniface, Manitoba. April 25, 1886. His last words to the Government of Canada were: "Do not mistreat my people."*

One Arrow is buried in Winnipeg on the ground of the St. Boniface Basilica. ✦

# 1885-1977

## DR. FREDERICK VALENTINE BIRD

In 1913 Boissevain was a bustling prairie community with almost all the amenities and services required in a town of less than 1,000 people. There was, however, a real need for a doctor prepared to make a long term commitment to the area. At the same time, among the graduating class at the Manitoba Medical College was a young man anxious to put his years of study into practice, and so began a relationship that was to last 60 years.

Frederick Valentine Bird was born north of Winnipeg on August 30, 1885, near old St. Andrews Church. He was the eighth of eleven children, and the third generation to be born in Manitoba. Bird's great-grandfather and grandfather both married Aboriginal wives, and his mother was the daughter of Scottish and Aboriginal parents. Although intensely proud of his mixed heritage, he spoke of it infrequently.

Even as a teenager Bird was attracted to the study of medicine. What had been an inclination, however, became a determination when his mother asked him to help her prepare a herbal medicine. After returning from the bush with the herb he had been sent to find Bird prepared a potion, which he later said must have contained digitalis, that his mother drank to cure her heart condition.

Bird wanted to attend the Manitoba Medical College when he graduated from high school, but a lack of money dictated that he become a teacher. After teaching for almost three years he saved enough money to begin medical studies. In the spring of 1913 he graduated with honours and promptly caught the train for Boissevain. The few basic instruments he brought with him allowed him to begin his practice, and on May 19th he saw his first patient.

Bird cared deeply for his community and its people, and spent hours every month serving on various boards and committees. In addition, he was for forty years the area's medical health officer, a town councilor (1924-29), mayor (1929-40) and again a councilor (until 1944). Bird was also a life-long Anglican and served St. Matthew's Anglican Church in various capacities. Fundraising for and refurbishing the church were, however, his pet projects. In addition, he served on the Board of Directors of Brandon College during some of its most trying times.

It is difficult to imagine that, with a family he loved dearly, a busy medical practice and an active involvement in community affairs, Bird had time for a hobby. He quickly earned a reputation in Boissevain, however, for his "green thumb," and his grounds were the horticultural showplace of the town. One fall he lifted 3,000 tulip bulbs and in 1967 he gave the town fifty sugar maple saplings he had raised from seed. He was also instrumental in redevelopment of the cemetery, following its acquisition from private interests.

The stock market crash of 1929 and the years that followed had a devastating impact on Bird. He once noted that he "practised through the dirty thirties, 1930 to 1940, by borrowing on my life insurance and finally on my home. While I continued to deliver babies the Farmers Credit Arrangement Board claimed my accounts were 'unsecured' and my business accounts were wiped out. I was $5000 in debt, my home was mortgaged and I had no assets. My first 27 years of medical practice were wiped out."

Near the end of his life Bird decided that he wanted his medical books, instruments and examining table given to an Aboriginal community. He did not, however, want Indian Affairs involved, since he felt that government bureaucracy would practically guarantee that his things would never reach the people who needed them. As a result, his equipment was turned over to the Dakota Ojibway Tribal Council, to be used wherever needed.

For his years of dedicated service to the people and community of Boissevain, Bird received a number of accolades, not least of which was the Manitoba Good Citizenship Award. A final recognition was tendered to his memory on July 5, 1977, when hundreds of his friends and admirers assembled to celebrate his life and passing.

In his eulogy Bird's son Clayton said that "A great — and what is far better — a good man has passed on, leaving the community a memory which it will long cherish and an example that will not lack emulation by young and generous souls following in his footsteps."

Dr. Frederick Valentine Bird is buried in the Boissevain cemetery. ✦

# 1863-1931

## DR. ROBERT STIRTON THORNTON

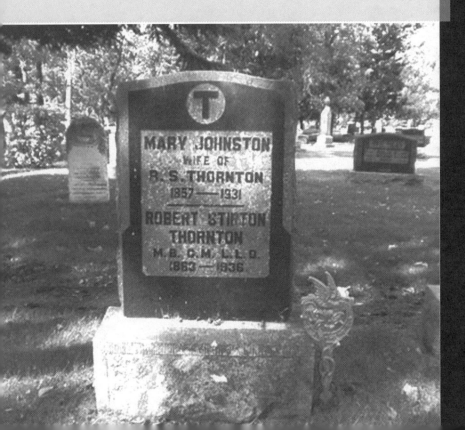

MARY JOHNSTON
WIFE OF
R. S. THORNTON
1857 — 1931
ROBERT STIRTON
THORNTON
M.B. C.M. L.L.D.
1863 — 1936

**A**n old if somewhat dated adage suggests that behind every successful man there is a caring, supportive woman. The same might be said of the growth and development of prairie communities in western Canada. Behind almost every successful town and village there was an insightful, giving and community-minded person, able to inspire others with her or his vision. And so it was with Deloraine's Dr. Thornton.

Robert Stirton Thornton was born in Edinburgh, Scotland on 8 May 1863. He attended the prestigious George Heriot's School before graduating from the University of Edinburgh with a medical degree. He immediately immigrated to Canada, arriving in Deloraine in 1887 as the region's first doctor.

Like most pioneer medical practitioners, Thornton attended to the needs of both members of his local community and settlers living in outlying areas. This meant coping with often impassable prairie trails, fierce winter blizzards and eighteen hour work days. For forty years this was the role played by "the doctor," a term of endearment used by family and friends.

Thornton's professional interests extended well beyond his local medical practice. In addition to serving as health officer for the Rural Municipality of Winchester, he was for a time president of the Medical Council of Manitoba and later, the Medical Council of Canada. His keen interest in his profession made him well known throughout Canada, and his reputation was acknowledged when Queen's University awarded him an honourary doctorate.

Apart from medicine, Thornton took a keen interest in politics, first as a member of his local town school board, and beginning in 1907, as Liberal member of the provincial legislature for Deloraine. After being defeated in 1910 Thornton won successive victories in 1914 and 1915, before entering the cabinet of premier Tobias C. Norris as Minister of Education. In that capacity he made a number of controversial decisions, not least of which was eliminating public funding of francophone schools. Although re-elected in 1920, the doctor was defeated two years later and retired from provincial politics.

Thornton's community activities were not limited to medicine, politics or the local Presbyterian church, on whose board he sat as an advocate of union with the Methodists. He was also an enthusiastic supporter of sports, particularly golf, curling and tennis. It was largely due to his efforts that *Outdoor Magazine* said "While we see many tennis courts in the west, treeless and open to the winds, such is not the case in Deloraine. Here is a pleasant tree sheltered place for both the players and the spectators alike."

Thornton was an active member of a number of fraternal organizations, including the Masons. In 1893-94 and 1896 he was Worshipful Master of the Deloraine Lodge, and in 1900 became Grand Master of the Grand Lodge of Manitoba, whose jurisdiction included the North-West Territories, Calgary and Edmonton.

Thornton's love for Deloraine and the surrounding countryside was evident in his determination to make the area an island of beauty in an otherwise treeless prairie. In addition to planting trees on his own property he encouraged his friends and neighbors to do likewise, earning Deloraine its reputation as the "town of trees."

When a two block parcel of railroad property became available for purchase an agreement between the town and the railway saw it developed with paths and manicured lawns and hedges, all designed by the doctor. Even in the busiest of times Thornton was often found overseeing town workers in the beautification project. His efforts did not go unnoticed, however, as national newspaper and magazine articles regularly referred to Deloraine as a prairie beauty spot.

Renovations to the town's cemetery were a particular passion of Thornton's. After years of neglect he was determined to make the cemetery a place of contemplation and tranquility, with every tree and shrub carefully planted and cared for. The Thornton home was another of his most personal projects, and over the years it became a centre of Deloraine's social life, with countless functions hosted by the doctor and his wife Mary.

After a car accident in 1931 ended the life of his wife, Thornton gave up his practice and retired to Victoria, British Columbia, where he died five years later. His body, however, was returned to Deloraine where it now rests beside that of his wife in the community to which he gave so much. ✦

• Dr. R.S. Thornton

# 1825-1913

## ELEANOR ELIZA CRIPPS (KENNEDY)

The life of Eleanor Eliza Cripps was both extraordinary and typical of many women and men who settled in pre-Confederation Manitoba. Born into an upper-class English family, she ended her life in Virden, the widow of a Métis husband who died penniless, despite at one time owning more than 17,000 acres of prairie farmland.

Eleanor Cripps was born on 2 November 1825 in London, England. She was fluent in languages, well read, and possessed of an aptitude for music and the ability to both sew and embroider. Yet, at the relatively advanced age of thirty-four she married the son of a Hudson Bay Company chief factor.

William Kennedy earned an international reputation after he was hired as commander of Lady Franklin's second expedition in search of her lost husband, Sir John Franklin. Although Kennedy's Arctic expedition was regarded by contemporaries as the best prepared of any to that date, it almost ended in disaster. Kennedy and four of his men were separated from their ship because of a shift in the ice, and the men were marooned for more than a month before being rescued. That and a second attempt by Kennedy to find Franklin both failed.

Two years after her marriage to William, they raised sufficient money to leave their home and travel as Church of England missionaries to the largely unsettled lands bordering Lake Manitoba. Exhausted after a difficult journey by ship, stagecoach, canoe and steamer, the couple rested in the Red River settlement for three months while waiting for the birth of their first child. When they finally arrived at their missionary outpost their church work included teaching Natives the gospel, as well as carpentry, blacksmithing and how to use farm implements.

Within a year of their arrival William's failing health forced them to give up their missionary work. Their return to England, however, was interrupted by a Sioux uprising in Minnesota, and the two were forced to return to the Red River settlement. In 1863 Eleanor gave birth to a daughter, and with the death of Kennedy's mother the two became the owners of a lot in St. Andrews, on which they built an attractive stone house they called Maple Grove.

The Kennedy's imported a piano, the second to arrive in the settlement, and began hosting regular musical evenings. Eleanor quickly became a popular performer and a respected choir director and organist at St Andrew's Church. One of her admirers was the future Anglican bishop of Qu'Appelle, who referred to his parishioner as the community's only "prima donna." Eleanor was variously described by others as a large woman of striking beauty, and because of her background, "the Duchess."

The Kennedys were respected community leaders, in no small measure

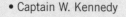

• Captain W. Kennedy

because of the work carried out by Eleanor in arranging concerts and in sewing clothes for those in need. During the Riel unrest which preceded Manitoba's entry into Confederation they were among a number of prominent community members who petitioned the Métis leader to spare the life of the English Protestants he was holding captive.

In the early 1870s William's health forced him to remain in bed for days on end. Eleanor, who was already teaching music, and William's brother, attempted to make ends meet by opening a small import business. The stylish clothing they brought from London and Paris immediately attracted customers from well beyond the settlement's boundaries. Their business took a turn for the worse, however, when William regained his health. He started importing inferior products and business quickly fell off. The Kennedys were forced to sell their store and, although William had acquired 17,000 acres of land by way of payment for the goods he sold, most of it became worthless when the Manitoba land boom ended.

William died in January 1890 and the following year Eleanor moved to Virden with her daughter. There she became well-known as an artist, poet and organist at St Mary's Church. In the summer of 1913 the former lay missionary injured herself in a fall, and she died on October 4th. Although her funeral was held in Virden, Eleanor was buried alongside her husband in St. Andrews Cemetery, north of Winnipeg. ◆

• Eleanor E. Cripps

# 1863-1962

## CHARLES A. SHANKEY

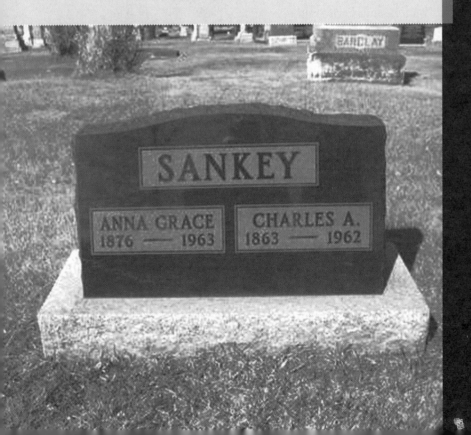

SANKEY

ANNA GRACE
1876 — 1963

CHARLES A.
1863 — 1962

The life story of Charles Sankey could be the stuff of fiction, starting on the heaving deck of the most famous ship in nautical history and ending nearly a century later in a small southern Manitoba town that he helped establish.

Sankey was born in Ireland on June 16, 1863. He was sixteen when he joined the merchant marine, and five days after returning to England from his first voyage he joined the crew of the Cutty Sark as a senior apprentice.

That clipper ship was commissioned by Jock Williams, a Scottish businessman, and built in 1869 in shipyards on the River Clyde. The name Cutty Sark came from the old Scots term for 'short nightshirt,' and is referred to in Robert Burn's famous poem Tam O'Shanter. Although designed as a cargo carrier, the 280-foot ship was also built for speed. Its long, narrow hull and thirty-six foot beam, together with more than 30,000 square feet of sails and eighteen kilometres of rigging, gave it one of the most distinctive nautical silhouettes of its time.

Sankey was a member of the Cutty Sark's twenty-eight man crew for two years, a period when a typical work day was more than twelve hours long and living conditions unbearably cramped. In retrospect, therefore, some of the crew were unhappy with their lot, so that during Sankey's last voyage a mutiny broke out, taking the life of a crew member and causing the Cutty Sark's captain to commit suicide. According to Sankey, it was then that he was made the ship's navigator and asked to guide the Cutty Sark home through the treacherous Java Strait.

When the ship eventually reached New York Sankey left the merchant marine to join members of his family in Toronto. His stay was brief, and he quickly left Ontario for his brothers' farm in the Boissevain area. He soon took up his own homestead and acquired a herd of cattle. In 1894 he sold his holdings and entered the Ontario Veterinary College at Guelph, graduating as gold medalist.

After working in the United States for three years as a cattle inspector Sankey returned to the Boissevain area to set up a veterinary practice. Two years later he learned that the Canadian Pacific Railway was extending its line from Deloraine to the newly surveyed town site of Waskada. Sankey was enthused about moving further west, and as soon as the rail line was completed he shipped his future residence and clinic, in the form of seven car-loads of lumber, to the community that was to be his home for the rest of his life.

Throughout his career Sankey was active in the life and growth of Waskada. He spent thirty-two years on the town's school board, twenty-five years as secretary of the Rural Municipality of Brenda, and served thirty-five years as a village councillor.

In 1905 the former sailor was asked to act as Paymaster and Enforcer of By-Laws. While serving in that capacity he saw the potential of thirty acres of unused land owned by the Canadian Pacific Railway. He became determined to construct on the acreage a beautifully landscaped multi-use park that would contain both a race track and ball park, along with hundreds of shrubs and trees.

After being assured that the land would be owned by the community in perpetuity, the CPR approved its sale for $30.00 per acre, and development began. In 1962 a large stone marker was unveiled in the park, and an embedded bronze plaque now describes the contributions made by Charles Sankey.

Sankey's children have followed in their father's footsteps. His daughter Mabel Pounder, for instance, bequeathed her oil rights on a half section of land to the town of Waskada "to be used for extra curricular education purposes, cemetery upkeep and town beautification generally."

In the early 1960s other family members established the Sankey Scholarship Fund to provide an annual award to deserving Grade 11 and 12 students.

Charles Sankey was married twice. He and Anna Josephine Ponton were the parents of one son, and following the death of his wife Sankey married Anna Grace McGill. The one-time mariner then became the father of a second son and two daughters.

Sankey was ninety-nine when he died in 1962. He is buried in the Waskada cemetery beside his second wife.

In a sad postscript to the Sankey story a devastating fire ripped through the de-commissioned Cutty Sark in the

Two years later he learned that the Canadian Pacific Railway was extending its line from Deloraine to the newly surveyed town site of Waskada.

early morning hours of May 21st, 2007. The historic ship had been encased in a stone dry-dock at Greenwich since the early 1990s, and just under thirty million dollars had been set aside for its restoration.

Although the fire destroyed the Cutty Sark's main and lower decks, many of its most valuable artifacts, including its figurehead, sails, mast and prow, had already been placed in storage.

According to the chief executive of the Cutty Sark Trust, the ship will be re-built, and its complex, curved design, compared by some to New York's famous Guggenheim museum, will again be seen by tourists who for more than forty years have been lining up to tour the world's last surviving tea clipper. ✦

THE LIFE STORIES DESCRIBED IN THIS CHAPTER are of six quite remarkable men, all of whom made an indelible impression on their respective communities. Harry Cater was Brandon's longest serving mayor. Thomas Mayne Daly and Francis Cornish were near contemporaries, and each was the first mayor of his adopted city. Stanley McInnis and John Davidson were both important members of the Legislative Assembly of Manitoba. McInnis is even now regarded as one of Manitoba's most popular politicians ever, while Davidson is among the few Canadians to found a town and then represent it on both the local and provincial level. Last but by no means least is Sir Clifford Sifton, the man credited with opening western Canada to settlement.

# CHAPTER 2

# politics

# 1852-1903

## JOHN ANDREW DAVIDSON

Although Manitoba has a long history of pioneer settlement, only one pioneer actually built his own town and then lived long enough to see it flourish as arguably the province's most attractive community. John Andrew Davidson was many things, including businessman, justice of the peace, sportsman, office holder and politician, but most significantly, he was the founder of Neepawa.

Davidson was born on 19 August 1852 in Thamesford, Upper Canada (now Ontario). In 1871 he and his family were part of the first group of Ontario immigrants to settle in Palestine, Manitoba. Two years later the twenty-one year-old Davidson established the first general store in the community, now known as Gladstone. Like most late 19th century storekeepers he accepted farm produce in exchange for the goods he sold, primarily because a lack of railway access made marketing agricultural products difficult. For a time the entrepreneurial young man also traded in furs, one of the few ventures in his long career in business which was unsuccessful.

Davidson quickly became a prominent member of his community, and within five years of his arrival in Gladstone he was a justice of the peace, commissioner for taking affidavits, trustee for the local school board and secretary of the Palestine Baseball Club. His hard work and altruism, however, did not translate into electoral success. When Westbourne was incorporated as a rural municipality he finished last in the area's first local elections.

In 1880 Davidson left Gladstone with Jonathan Joseph Hamilton for Beautiful Plains, where the two built the core of an entirely new town. In addition to their own brick building they constructed Neepawa's first hotel, flour-mill, blacksmith's shop, real estate office and a variety of other businesses, all in an effort to attract settlers. Their gamble paid off. When Neepawa was incorporated in November 1883, the town had 308 residents.

Almost overnight Davidson became one of the region's wealthiest and most influential businessmen. He was president of the Neepawa Mining Company, the Register Printing Company and the Neepawa Curling Club, and a member of town council.

His interest in politics, however, extended beyond the Beautiful Plains district. When the province's western boundary was extended west in 1881 he became the first member of the newly created constituency of Dauphin. Two years later he was re-elected by acclamation. His first two campaigns as a Conservative candidate in his home region were not as successful, and he was defeated in 1886 and 1888.

• J.A. Davidson

Whatever euphoria he might have felt following his sixteen vote victory in the following general election did not last long. In 1894 his seat was voided and in the ensuing by-election he was defeated. Although he also lost in the next two elections, when Hugh John Macdonald became the Conservative premier of Manitoba in 1900 the Liberal member for Beautiful Plains was persuaded to resign so that Davidson could enter the new cabinet as Provincial Treasurer, Minister of Agriculture and Provincial Lands Commissioner.

He is buried in Neepawa's Riverside Cemetery below a headstone immortalized by Margaret Laurence as 'the Stone Angel.'

Davidson quickly mastered the intricacies of finance, and by the end of his first year in office he had retired the entire deficit built up under the administration of outgoing Liberal premier Thomas Greenway. His succeeding two budgets both resulted in a provincial surplus, largely because of the new tax he imposed on the province's corporations.

Davidson's death in 1903 came at the end of a lengthy period of poor health. Around 9:00 am on the 14th of November the fifty-one year old politician awoke from a deep sleep to see his bed surrounded by family members. After saying a brief goodbye, he closed his eyes and died. Within an hour Neepawa's town bell tolled his passing and flags were lowered to half-mast.

Four days later a special train carrying members of the Manitoba legislature and other dignitaries arrived to pay tribute to one of the province's best known and most respected pioneers. Shortly before noon on the day of his funeral, Davidson's body was moved from his home to the Methodist Church, where it lay in state in the hours before his services. As mourners entered for what one observer called the largest if shortest funeral in Neepawa's history, they saw dozens of floral wreaths arranged below a choir loft and a pulpit draped in black.

Following the services Davidson's body was transported north to the town's cemetery, closely followed by a procession of mourners extending more than a half mile behind. Davidson was survived by his wife, two sons and three daughters. He is buried in Neepawa's Riverside Cemetery below a headstone immortalized by Margaret Laurence as 'the Stone Angel.' ✦

HARRY WILLIAM CATER

DEC. 4, 1869 — APR. 3, 1945.

ELIZA JANE CATER

AUG. 15, 1882 — JAN. 29, 1967.

# 1869-1945

## HARRY WILLIAM CATER

**M**anitoba historian Lee Clark referred to him as the personific-ation of a successful municipal politician, and he was mayor of Brandon for a period longer than any of the city's other twenty-nine chief magistrates.

Harry William Cater, born in Norfolk, England, in 1869, emigrated to Ontario as an eighteen-year-old. He moved to Brandon from St. Thomas in 1889 and within four years took over the pump manufacturing business with which he remained associated throughout his life.

When Cater first ran for mayor in 1913 he styled himself the voice of the workingman. During his campaign he strongly criticized the city's decision to reduce the wages of its 300 member workforce, insisted that a "fair wage" clause be inserted in all civic contracts, and proposed a five and one-half day work week. Brandon voters had their choice between Cater, the friend of the working class, and Alderman Joseph Hughes, one of the city's most influential businessmen.

Cater lost, but in 1914 he ran again. When Mayor Hughes announced that he would not seek a second term, the chairman of the city's finance committee became the establishment candidate, and it was he who voters held accountable for the failed promises and misdeeds of the previous administration. Hughes had said he

On the cover of his 1915 diary the new mayor listed his qualifications for public office as "1. Honesty 2. Capacity 3. Experience 4. Tact."

would reduce taxes, but they had gone up, a civic survey carried out by the city was described as "a huge and costly joke," and hundreds of electors were prevented from casting a ballot because of a mix-up in the voters' list. Ultimately, all Cater had to do was remind Brandonites that he was not "a Rosser Avenue candidate."

On the cover of his 1915 diary the new mayor listed his qualifications for public office as "1. Honesty 2. Capacity 3. Experience 4. Tact." In reality, however, it was World War I that most contributed to his early political success. Certainly his uncontested 1915 victory was due to the willingness of voters to put aside ideological differences in a time of war. But that sense of unity came to a dramatic end the following year. The issue of Daylight Savings Time, and a suggestion that the debt of the YMCA be off-loaded onto local tax-payers, divided the city along class lines. Nonetheless, Cater was again re-elected.

By 1918 relations between Cater and members of his council had deteriorated to the point that the *Brandon*

*Sun* suggested that the main obstacle to the city's growth was "the Mayor's attitude towards civic business." Cater's mayoral opponent this time was Reginald McDiarmid, a member of a well-known city family and president of the local Board of Trade. Few were surprised when Cater was defeated by over 200 votes.

The 1919 mayoral election pitted Cater against George Dinsdale, whose son Walter was to serve in the federal cabinet of John Diefenbaker. Dinsdale Sr. was a well-respected businessman, and he and most colleagues spoke loudly of Brandon's future and the growth that would be coming the city's way. On the other hand, members of the city's working class felt that they already had been victimized by the war effort, and were no longer prepared to pay a disproportionate share of the cost of running the city. Once again the choice was clear, and Cater, the labour candidate, was easily beaten by the development vote.

By 1921, however, economic and political considerations had changed. Taxes had risen and the city's debt load had become a matter of grave concern to voters. This time Cater attracted the support of most of Brandon's business community, and he returned to office for what turned out to be an uninterrupted decade in power.

Much of Cater's political success can be attributed to either his strong sense of conviction or his stubborness,

In 1937 the *Brandon Sun* referred to him as "the dictator of ruinous policies," and he was easily defeated by Frederick Young, a man he had twice previously beaten.

depending on whether you were a supporter. When he and city aldermen were not of the same mind on an issue he was likely to abruptly adjourn a meeting, declare a motion "out of order," or exercise his power of veto. In one instance, when his veto was over-ruled, he sat in the visitors' gallery and continued to verbally harass members of his council.

Cater's second stint in office ended in 1931. In that year the impact of the Depression was everywhere evident, including Brandon, where in one year the number of city families on relief rose by a staggering 871%. Just before the municipal election six hundred people attended a meeting of the Brandon Progress Association, an organization devoted to defeating Cater. Slightly more than 4,000 Association supporters went to the polls, easily guaranteeing the victory of ex-alderman Edward Fotheringham, yet another city businessman.

To the surprise of even his most ardent supporters, the political career of Harry Cater was far from over. In 1933 he won what was now a two-year term, and in 1935 he earned another. Cater's time, however, was rapidly winding down, and he could no longer escape responsibility for Brandon's sorry economic condition. In 1937 The *Brandon Sun* referred to him as "the dictator of ruinous policies," and he was easily defeated by Frederick Young, a man he had twice previously beaten.

Although Cater was a candidate for alderman in 1938, and a candidate for mayor the following year, in the end he was vanquished by a force even he could not conquer: time. Harry William Cater, whose successes and defeats mirrored Brandon's up-and-down fortunes, died on April 3rd, 1945. The father of five is buried in the Brandon cemetery beside Eliza Jane, his wife of thirty-eight years. ✦

# 1831-1878

## FRANCIS EVANS CORNISH

**B**efore and after he died Francis Evans Cornish had been described as a dandy, a political fixer and a rogue. Although popular, he was accused by opponents of bigamy, assault, drunkenness, and boisterousness. Despite his faults, Winnipeg's first mayor epitomized the brawling and often bigoted ideology of frontier Manitoba.

Cornish was born in the London district of what in 1831 was know as Upper Canada. Twenty-four years later he was called to the bar, and in 1861 elected London's seventh mayor. Despite accusations of ballot box stuffing and political chicanery, he was re-elected in each of the next two years. According to critics his success was less due to his personal popularity than the fact that, in each of his successful elections, he had arranged for British soldiers to be stationed in the city the day before an election so that the following day they could vote for him. By 1864, however, members of his council had had enough, and they called out the militia to supervise that year's election. Cornish lost, and eight years later he left for Winnipeg.

After pleading guilty he fined himself four dollars, then reached into one of his pockets and removed the money. He accepted it on behalf of the city, and dropped it into a second pocket.

• Francis Evans Cornish

While mayor of London Cornish earned a well-founded reputation for drinking. In the 1860s a mayor automatically became his community's police magistrate. Consequently, when Cornish was arrested for public drunkenness he presided over his own trial. After pleading guilty he fined himself four dollars, then reached into one of his pockets and removed the money. He accepted it on behalf of the city, and dropped it into a second pocket. He concluded by lecturing himself on the evils of drink.

In Winnipeg he immediately set up a law practice and became active in politics. He had left behind his wife but not his bad habits, and he was soon a leader of Manitoba's ultra-Protestant anti-Francophone movement. Winnipeg in 1872 was still very much a frontier community, and it was not unusual for men like Cornish to take matters into their hands. So it was that within weeks of his arrival in the province he and a group of equally drunk followers ransacked a St. Boniface polling station because the newcomers had been denied the right to vote. This should not have come as a surprise since they had not lived in the settlement long enough to satisfy the city's residency requirements.

On a separate occasion Cornish and his followers attacked a group of unarmed Métis with wooden wheel spokes before retreating to Winnipeg. There he climbed onto a wagon and in a speech fuelled equally by liquor and bigotry, he insulted the province's lieutenant governor, its sheriff and the head of the Hudson's Bay Company before concluding by referring to Winnipeg's police chief as a "toad-eating Communist."

Three hundred and eighty-eight residents were entitled to vote in Winnipeg's first election. When the ballots were counted in January 1874, Cornish had received 383 votes to his opponent's 179. Although the new mayor was accused of stuffing the ballot boxes, apparently a skill he had learned in Ontario, nothing was proven. When charged with fomenting violence during the 1876 municipal election, however, he was convicted and fined twenty dollars (a significant sum at the time) for his role in a riot that he had started. In another incident he kidnapped his opponent on the eve of an election, brought charges of corruption against him, and then stated that the failure of his opponent to come forward to answer the charges amounted to a confession of guilt.

As in Ontario in the 1860s, Manitoba mayors in the 1870s also sat as police magistrates. In a case reminiscent of his experience in London, Cornish was sitting as magistrate when he was accused of having been drunk while driving his horse and buggy the previous evening. Stepping down from the bench, he turned his back towards those sitting in his courtroom and faced his now empty chair. He admitted that yes, the charge was true, and he entered a plea of guilty. He then fined himself five dollars, but suspended the sentence on the grounds that it was his first offence.

Although Cornish was popular with the Protestant, English-speaking Ontario immigrants who flooded into

the province after Manitoba's entry into Confederation, his outlandish behaviour and crude language offended politicians in Winnipeg and Ottawa alike. Prime Minister John A. Macdonald, who also had a rough edge as a politician, even went so far as to ask the province's lieutenant governor to indict him criminally for his many acts of election violence.

Although a member of the provincial legislature since 1872, Cornish re-entered civic politics as a Winnipeg alderman but then died of stomach cancer in November 1878. He was forty-seven. The only mention of his passing in the province's newspapers was a brief announcement placed in the *Manitoba Free Press* by his family.

Francis Evans Cornish, the first mayor of Winnipeg and arguably this province's most colourful politician, is buried in Winnipeg's Brookside Cemetery. ✦

> Although the new mayor was accused of stuffing the ballot boxes, apparently a skill he had learned in Ontario, nothing was proven.

# 1865-1907

## STANLEY WILLIAM McINNIS

Although there is no way to know for sure, a Brandon dentist died one of the most publicized deaths in the province's history, as newspapers in banner headlines daily reported first his declining health and then his passing.

Stanley William McInnis was born in Saint John, New Brunswick, in 1865 and moved as a youth with his family to Manitoba. In 1888 he graduated from the Philadelphia Dental College to become Manitoba's first college-educated dentist. The following year he established his practice in Brandon and embarked on a remarkable series of accomplishments. He was a founding member of the Canadian Dental Association and the organization's first registrar. He was also instrumental in the establishment of the Dominion Dental Council, a national body created to set common licensing standards, and twice served as president of the Manitoba Dental Association.

On a local level he was a director of the Brandon Board of Trade and the Western Agricultural and Arts Association of Manitoba, president of the Provincial Game Protective Association, the Brandon Horticultural Society and president of a number of Brandon clubs, including the Gun Club, the Brandon Athletic Club and the Brandon Turf Club. In 1899 the popular dentist scored a

McInnis' "breadth of thought, independence of view, and freedom from petty ideas made him an ornament to the legislature and a valued asset in the public life of Manitoba."
— *Manitoba Free Press*

• Stanley W. McInnis

huge political upset to enter the Manitoba legislature as the Conservative member for Brandon City. He was re-elected twice, and in 1907 was appointed Provincial Secretary and the Minister for Education in Manitoba.

Always affable and courteous, McInnis made friends easily and according to the *Manitoba Free Press,* his "breadth of thought, independence of view, and freedom from petty ideas made him an ornament to the legislature and a valued asset in the public life of Manitoba."

In late October 1907 McInnis had just joined a group of his friends at the Oak Lake Shooting Club when he suffered an attack of appendicitis. His condition quickly worsened and he was rushed to the Brandon Hospital. By the time he was operated on his appendix had burst, his bowel had been perforated and blood poisoning had set in. Front page

headlines in the *Manitoba Free Press* made it clear his condition was hopeless: "DR. M'INNIS DEATH HOURLY EXPECTED, Provincial Secretary in Brandon Hospital — No Hope of Recovery."

Although his burst appendix left him paralyzed below the waist, McInnis not only regained consciousness, he was lucid up to the moment of his death. Told by his doctors that he had only hours to live, he methodically began putting his affairs in order. First he sent for his business partner and a stenographer, and when they arrived he dictated a series of letters and memoranda. Next he called his lawyer and added a codicil to his will. When that was done he met with Premier Rodmond Roblin, who along with cabinet ministers Robert Rogers and Colin Campbell had arrived in Brandon shortly after they had been advised of his deteriorating condition.

Without emotion McInnis told his friend and mentor that he had only a handful of hours to live, and that he would be comforted if the premier promised to complete the changes begun in the two departments under his stewardship. Roblin agreed to ensure that they were carried out. After the premier left his room McInnis again sent for the stenographer. When she arrived he dictated a letter of farewell to the citizens of Brandon, ending it with "That heaven prosper the fair city of Brandon, and all the kind friends in it, is my parting wish." That done, the stricken dentist discussed with those surrounding his bed his impending death. He said that, although he could feel the poison gradually spreading upwards, he was in no pain.

As she had during his entire hospital stay, Clara Beckwith McInnis sat by her dying husband. Spectators were deeply moved by the sight of the two quietly talking as if nothing unusual was happening. Joining Clara at the end were one of the dentist's brothers, two city aldermen and two of her husband's doctors. Speaking to the group McInnis

Speaking to the group McInnis spoke of the sensation of dying. "I hear something ringing in my ears. I feel something coming. Goodbye."

spoke of the sensation of dying. "I hear something ringing in my ears. I feel something coming. Goodbye." With that the life of the forty-two year-old Stanley William McInnis came to an end.

While there is no record of the words which passed between McInnis and his wife as he lay on his deathbed, the ever pragmatic dentist may well have spoken to his wife of Christina Rossetti's poem 'When I Am Dead, My Dearest':

When I am dead, my dearest,
Sing no sad songs for me;
Plant thou no roses at my head,
Nor shady cypress tree:
Be the green grass above me
With showers and dewdrops wet;
And if thou wilt, remember,
And if thou wilt, forget. ✦

# 1852-1911

## THOMAS MAYNE DALY

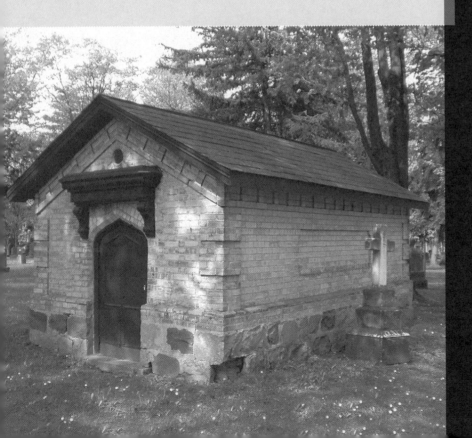

In pioneer communities someone, or an entire family, will often accomplish something significant. Few people, however, have won as many accolades as Thomas Mayne Daly, Brandon's first mayor and the nation's first juvenile court judge.

Born in 1852 in Stratford, Canada West, to a family of considerable affluence, his paternal great-grandfather was a senior officer in the British navy, and his grandfather prospered as a Stratford businessman and the city's first mayor. Daly's father was also a prominent man of business, and twice elected mayor.

Daly Jr. was educated at Upper Canada College in Toronto and called to the Ontario bar in 1876. For the next five years he practised law in his home town. He was a big, burly, good-natured man of immense charm. Although he carried himself with an erect, military bearing he never took himself too seriously, and was well-known for his wit and amusing anecdotes.

In a speech delivered in Brandon, Canada's first prime minister once said "I am told that some in this country are not content, but you know, ladies and gentlemen, some of us will not be content in heaven if we hear of a place farther west." That was certainly the case with Daly. In the spring of 1881 he traveled to Winnipeg and then up the Assiniboine River by flatboat to Brandon, where he arrived on July 18th. He became a solicitor the following year and a barrister in 1884, dividing time between practising law and selling real estate.

Daly brought to Manitoba an abiding interest in politics. When Brandon was incorporated on May 30th, 1882, he became the city's first mayor, and although he was defeated by William Winter the following year, he won a second term in 1884.

Daly was also a candidate in four national elections. In 1887, while still living in Brandon, he was defeated in the federal constituency of Selkirk. Four years later, however, he was successful, and on 17 October 1892 he was sworn as Minister of the Interior and Superintendent of Indian Affairs in the administration of Sir John Abbott. He thus became the first politician from Manitoba to sit in a federal cabinet.

Abbott resigned as prime minister a month later and was followed in office by John Thompson, who kept Daly in cabinet. Two years later Thompson died, and his successor also kept him on. Mackenzie Bowell, however, was arguably Canada's weakest prime minister, and less than two years after forming a government he was forced to resign by a group of disgruntled cabinet members led by Sir Charles Tupper. Perhaps because he refused to join the conspiracy, Daly was not invited to join Tupper's cabinet. Disappointed and disillusioned, he refused to run in the 1896 general election.

• Daly's funeral cortege in Winnipeg

Daly had moved to Winnipeg in 1892, but when he left politics he settled in Rossland, British Columbia. At the time Rossland was a flourishing silver mining community, its streets full of prospectors and entertainment, ranging from prize fights and gambling to orchestras that played twenty-four hours a day. Although Daly was appointed a police commissioner the year after his arrival, his enthusiasm for living in a mining town quickly waned. In 1902 he returned to Winnipeg, where he rapidly built a thriving law practice. Two years later he was appointed the city's police magistrate. In 1908, however, he resigned briefly to run against Clifford Sifton in the federal election. He lost by sixty-nine out of 7,000 votes cast and immediately returned to his old job.

On the bench Daly was kind but not soft-hearted. He was not reluctant to mete out severe sentences, though

Daly became the first juvenile court judge in Canadian history. Initially his court sat in the dining room of a Salvation Army hostel...

in doing so he was always fair, and he quickly earned the respect of those who appeared in front of him. That often included children, a fact which became a gnawing concern to Daly. Both privately and publicly he deplored the law dealing with juveniles. It gave magistrates only two options: they could either commit a child to an adult prison, or they could return the child to the same environment that gave rise to the criminal conduct in the first place.

In 1908, however, a bill to establish a separate jurisdiction for young offenders was introduced in parliament. Its focus was on rehabilitation rather than punishment, and it provided that no juvenile could be convicted of a crime. Instead, a child was to be regarded as a delinquent, and dealt with as "a misdirected and misguided child, and one needing aid, encouragement, help and assistance."

The following February Daly became the first juvenile court judge in Canadian history. Initially his court sat in the dining room of a Salvation Army hostel, but within a year it moved to a new three-storey brick building in which girls were housed on the second floor and boys on the third. To thwart night-time escapes inmates hung their clothes outside of their rooms, which were then locked from dusk to dawn.

Daly sat twice a week, but his court was different than the norm. Instead of a place of intimidation it was where he and young offenders talked things over. Children instinctively trusted him, and they spoke to him as they would to a friend. When not in court he routinely visited the homes of problem children to see if there was anything he could do to help their parents.

Late in the evening of 23 June 1911, Daly was sitting with his family on the verandah of their home when he was suddenly seized with intense pain. Around 5:00 am the next morning he died from what doctors suspected was an internal hemorrhage. He was fifty-nine.

In addition to being remembered as a politician, lawyer and judge Daly is remembered as the driving forced behind establishment of the Children's Hospital of Winnipeg, and as the author of the then definitive book on Canadian criminal procedure. In 1913 a Winnipeg street was named in his honour, and more recently his Brandon home has become a museum and municipal heritage site.

Thomas Mayne Daly was survived by his wife and their two sons. He is buried beside his family's mausoleum in Stratford's Avondale Cemetery. ◆

# 1861-1929

## SIR CLIFFORD SIFTON

Among Canadian politicians the most important for settlement of the west was Sir Clifford Sifton. One eastern newspaper referred to him as the young Napoleon of a part of Canada known more for its blighted promises than its great potential. He appeared on the political landscape at time when the prairies needed a firm leader, and he was certainly that. A man with strong opinions about everything, between 1896 and 1911 he was also member of parliament for Brandon.

Sifton was born on 10 March 1861 in Upper Canada. His father was a farmer, small oil producer and a strong supporter of the Liberal party. In 1874 Sifton Sr. was rewarded for his loyalty with contracts to build a telegraph line northwest of Winnipeg and sections of the Canada Pacific Railway east of Selkirk and west of Thunder Bay. The following year the Siftons moved to Manitoba.

Clifford attended college in Ontario but articled with a Winnipeg law firm. He was called to the Manitoba bar in 1882 and immediately moved to Brandon, at the time a city of tents, to establish a law practice which his elder brother soon joined. Six years later Sifton was elected to the Manitoba legislature from North Brandon and, by the time he resigned to run federally, he was the province's

Attorney General, Provincial Lands Commissioner and Minister of Education.

In 1896 Sifton entered parliament as Prime Minister Wilfrid Laurier's Minister of the Interior and Superintendent General of Indian Affairs. In the years preceding his appointment many of those homesteading on the prairies had been overwhelmed by the rigours of prairie life, and had packed up and moved to the United States. Sifton set out to reverse that trend.

Salaried immigration officials suddenly found theselves working for commission, based on the actual number of immigrants settling in the west. Three thousand agents were hired throughout the United States, and advertisements touting the attractiveness of land on the Canadian prairies were published in more than seven thousand American papers.

Once American immigrants began to move into the west Sifton shifted the focus of the government's immigration policy to eastern Europe. His policy of paying bonuses to Canadian land companies for every immigrant they delivered to the prairies was just one of the controversies with which he became associated. Many Canadians were horrified by the influx of Poles, Russians and Ukrainians. One newspaper even referred to Sifton's immigration policy as a round "of European Freaks and Hobboes." Despite this and other criticisms, the campaign was an outstanding success and the number of immigrants entering Canada rose from 16,835 in 1896 to 141,465 in 1905.

Sifton astounded the country with his abrupt resignation at the end of February 1905. He had become convinced that the education clauses in the bills intended to establish the provinces of Alberta and Saskatchewan extended to Roman Catholics privileges beyond those which they then possessed under previous territorial governments. When Laurier refused to compromise on the wording Sifton resigned. Other factors, however, influenced Sifton's decision. He had been passed over by Laurier for promotion,

Famous for his knowledge of back room politics and the use of patronage, charges of corruption dogged him his entire career.

and there were suggestions that he feared to face public charges of corruption and adultery. Neither charge was ever substantiated.

Sifton remained in parliament as a private member until 1911. In January of that year Laurier announced that his government would be entering into a reciprocity agreement with the United States. Sifton opposed the move, and although he decided not to run again for parliament, he agreed to join the Conservative anti-reciprocity campaign and to organize Ontario for the Conservatives. The Conservative's convincing victory was largely the result of Sifton's efforts, but his Brandon supporters and most of his former Liberal colleagues felt betrayed.

Sifton was knighted in 1915, and four years later he and his family moved to Toronto. In the last decade of his life he was deeply mistrusted by politicians of every stripe; but he was nevertheless contemplating a return to politics when he died of heart failure in New York City on 17 April 1929. He had been sitting in a chair talking to one of his sons when he suddenly grew quiet. He dropped his hand, told his son that he felt weak, and then leaned his head against the back of his chair and died. Sifton was buried three days later beside his wife and son, Winfield.

Sifton was always a controversial figure. Famous for his knowledge of back room politics and the use of patronage, charges of corruption dogged him his entire career. Even his critics, however, agreed that more than any other Canadian he was responsible for the settlement of western Canada.

Sir Clifford Sifton is buried in Toronto's Mount Pleasant Cemetery. ✦

**CHAPTER 3**

THE SEVEN MEN WHOSE LIVES ARE DESCRIBED in this chapter each have an important place in the historical record. Although Francis Chaplin was once one of Canada's most respected violinists, he is now better known as the mentor of an even more illustrious virtuoso; and while James Freer did not invent motion pictures, he was the first Canadian movie-maker. The fame of Paul Hiebert has also faded since he brought to life the Sweet Songstress of Saskatchewan, but he too is an important part of the cultural fabric. George Tackaberry, Sandy Graham and Bulldog Brown all occupy a significant niche in the evolution of their respective sports; Tackaberry because he invented the modern hockey skate, Graham because his death led to the creation of North America's Jockeys' Guild, and Brown because he was a wrestling role model.

# arts & leisure

# 1927-1993

## FRANCIS EUGENE CHAPLIN

I f teachers are judged by the excellence of their students, then the twentieth century's most accomplished pedagogue at Brandon University died tragically in the early hours of December 3, 1993.

Francis Eugene Chaplin was born in Newcastle, New Brunswick in 1927 and immediately established himself as a violin prodigy. The *Globe and Mail* described his Toronto debut as brilliant, a characterization repeated following the sixteen year-old's performances with the Calgary Philharmonic and the Regina and Edmonton symphonies.

Chaplin entered the Julliard School of Music in 1946 to study with Louis Persinger and Ivan Galamian. While a student in New York he spent five years as concertmaster of the Manhattan Chamber Orchestra and was a frequent soloist with orchestras along America's east coast. He graduated with the Morris Loeb Memorial Award, given to the student considered the most excellent in talent, ability and achievement.

Two years after Chaplin returned to Halifax the twenty-eight year old became concertmaster of the Halifax Symphony and the CBC Halifax Concert and Chamber Orchestra. That same year he also co-founded the Halifax Trio, which eventually became the Brandon Trio and one of the country's oldest chamber ensembles.

> As a soloist Chaplin toured extensively in Canada, performing with orchestras in Toronto, Calgary, Edmonton, the city of Quebec, Hamilton, Regina and New York.

As a soloist Chaplin toured extensively in Canada, performing with orchestras in Toronto, Calgary, Edmonton, the city of Quebec, Hamilton, Regina and New York. Among his many recordings were 10 Caprices for Solo Violin by S.C. Eckhardt-Gramatté and performances with Judy Loman and the Johnny Bart Orchestra.

Chaplin and his fellow trio members, Edward Bisha and Gordon Macpherson, came to Brandon University in 1966 as Artists-in-Residence, and all three stayed on to teach in the school's three year-old music program. Although the university's Department of Music was founded in 1906, the year Chaplin arrived Jack Spalding became the first student to graduate with a Bachelor of Music degree.

Chaplin was both a brilliant performer and an outstanding teacher, and in 1991 he was awarded the Brandon University Alumni Award for Excellence in Teaching. Among his students were Victor Schultz, Thomas Williams of McGill University and Maria Guidos-Albert, with the Timmins Symphony Orchestra.

Without a doubt James Ehnes is the most famous of his many brilliant students. Born in Brandon (1976), Ehnes began violin studies at the age of four and at nine became a protégé of Chaplin's. An eleven-year Ehnes gained national recognition as winner of the Grand Prize in Strings at the Canadian Music Competition, and the following year became the youngest musician to win the First Prize in Strings at the Canadian Music Festival. Ehnes made his orchestral solo debut with the Orchestre Symphonique de Montréal when he was thirteen, and subsequently studied at Juilliard. He graduated in 1997 with the Peter Mennin Prize for Outstanding Achievement and Leadership in Music and established an international reputation performing with such renowned conductors as Vladimir Ashkenazy, Sir Andrew Davis, Charles Dutoit and Bobby McFerrin. In 2005 Ehnes was awarded an honourary Doctor of Music degree by Brandon University.

Chaplin's career, and life, ended on the first Thursday in December, 1993. Around 5:30 am a city of Brandon employee plowing snow on 13th Street noticed flames inside the musician's three-storey brick house. Although firefighters managed to confine the blaze to the living room, by the time they arrived smoke had already spread throughout the remainder of the house. Chaplin was found unconscious in a smoke-filled upstairs bedroom and died shortly after being admitted to hospital. He was survived by his wife, son and daughter.

Ehnes has credited Chaplin with instilling in him the love of music, and Patrick Carrabre suggested that his deceased colleague set a standard for both musical excellence and personal integrity. In 1974 both were acknowledged by Mount Allison University, which awarded Chaplin an honourary doctorate in music.

Ironically, at the time of his death Chaplin and the Brandon Trio had been preparing the commissioned work Firebrand. He is buried in the Brandon Cemetery. ◆

FREER

# 1855-1933

## JAMES SIMMONS FREER

When movie enthusiasts discuss early Canadian filmmakers and actors they typically speak of Louis B. Mayer, Walter Pidgeon, Glenn Ford and actresses like Mary Pickford and Fay Wray. Few remember that this country's first filmmaker came from Brandon.

James Simmons Freer was born on January 4th 1855 in Woodstock, England. Thirty-three years later he was married, the father of six and working as a newspaper reporter in Bristol when he and his wife emigrated to Canada and settled on a farm in the hills ten miles south of Brandon. In 1901 he moved to a farm seven miles northeast of Elkhorn, where he remained for the next sixteen years.

The events which allowed Freer to make Canadian history actually started in the basement of a café on the Boulevard des Capucines in Paris in 1895. On December 28th brothers Auguste and Louis Lumiere gave the world's first public screening of a motion picture. In all they showed ten short films, each lasting about two minutes, using an instrument they called a 'cinematograph,' essentially a combination camera, projector and printer.

Two years later Freer purchased a similar device, manufactured by Thomas Edison, and in the fall of 1897 became Canada's first filmmaker. His short films were either of farm scenes or of trains

In England Freer promoted the value of Canadian agricultural pursuits, the richness of prairie soil and the free homesteads available to immigrants. His movies were arguably the first example of government sponsored media propaganda.

and, like the work of the Lumieres, they were less than two minutes long and their titles were an accurate description of their content. Freer's first films included "Typical Stooking Scene," "Six Binders at Work in a Hundred Acre Wheatfield," "Cyclone Thresher at Work" and "Arrival of CPR Express at Winnipeg."

As Freer became more comfortable with film-making his pictures became more sophisticated. Some combined shots of both farms and trains, like "Harvesting Scene, With Train Passing By," while others focused on politicians and children, like "Premier Greenway Stooking Grain" and "Coming 'thru' to Rye."

Freer filmed events which occurred both near his farm and elsewhere in Manitoba. He shot "Canadian Militia Charing Fortified Wall" because elements of the Canadian

military trained near his home. A frequent visitor to Winnipeg, he made films like "Winnipeg Fire Boys on the Warpath" and "Canadian Continental Jubilee."

The ability of this new medium to attract large crowds was quickly recognized by many of those with a message to convey. Among the most impressed were William Van Horne, the president of the Canadian Pacific Railway, and Clifford Sifton, the member of parliament for Brandon and federal Minister of the Interior. Both men became convinced that motion pictures were a much better way to promote the Canadian prairies to prospective immigrants than the traditional lantern slide shows.

The same year that Freer purchased his Edison camera/projector he persuaded Van Horne to fund a film and lecture tour of the British Isles, which he advertised as 'Ten Years in Manitoba — 25,000 instantaneous photos upon half-a-mile of Edison films.' For Freer the tour was a paid vacation, but for the railway company it was an opportunity to recruit people who would both buy CPR land in the west, and use their trains when traveling about Canada's vast expanse. In England Freer promoted the value of Canadian agricultural pursuits, the richness of prairie soil and the free homesteads available to immigrants. His movies were arguably the first example of government sponsored media propaganda.

Freer's tour was such a success that he stayed in England for more than a year. During that time he kept busy making the kinds of films that homesick English immigrants were most anxious to see. Typical was "The Changing Guards at St. James Palace."

When Freer returned to Manitoba in the spring of 1899 he immediately began making plans for a second tour of Britain. Whether too busy farming to make new films or simply because he ran out of energy, he started buying the films of others rather than making his own.

The first tour had been such a popular success that Sifton's ministry agreed to sponsor a second one. So in 1902 Freer headed back to Britain. This time, however, the trip was a disappointment. Many films he showed were made by others, their quality was not good, and Freer was now playing to a more informed audience. To make matters worse, he was also confronted by rumours that he either completely ignored, or at the very least played down, such as the freezing cold of prairie winters and the biting reality of Manitoba mosquitoes.

Freer's second tour of England was his last involvement with commercial film making. After 1902 the CPR took over direct financing of immigration films, and in a decision which over the next century was to become the reality of

Whether too busy farming to make new films or simply because he ran out of energy, he started buying the films of others rather than making his own.

the Canadian motion picture industry, it hired a foreign company to make films of Canada.

Freer returned to Elkhorn and abandoned movie-making entirely, although he continued to give the occasional film show locally. All that now remains of his films are a handful of copies in Ottawa's National Archive, and although he is credited with having made this country's first motion pictures, he has been largely forgotten.

In 1917 the Freers left Elkhorn for Winnipeg, where James began working for the *Winnipeg Free Press*. Freer died on December 23rd, 1933 and is buried in Elmwood Cemetery beside his wife and one of his sons. ✦

# 1892-1987

# PAUL GERHARDT HIEBERT

In the late 1940s a charming if irreverent university professor introduced the world to a prairie poet whose lyrical gifts and unerring sense of rhyme was to secure for herself an international reputation and, for her biographer, Canada's highest award for humour. For the past sixty years Sarah Binks has held Canadians in thrall with the tripping metre of works like "My Garden: A little blade of grass I see/ Its banner waving wild and free/And I wonder if in time to come/ 'Twill be a great big onion."

Paul Gerhardt Hiebert was born in 1892 at Pilot Mound, the sixth child of a family of seven sons and three daughters. He graduated from the University of Manitoba in 1916 before earning a Master's degree in Gothic and Teutonic philology from the University of Toronto, a Master's in science, and in 1924, a doctorate in chemistry from McGill. From that time until his retirement he was a professor at the University of Manitoba.

Hiebert began writing poetry as a child and continued to write until he was past ninety years of age. He loved to entertain. On the long streetcar rides to the university he delighted in reading aloud the latest bad poems sent to him by the fictional Sarah Binks. For years both undergrads and professors alike pressed him for

On the long streetcar rides to the university he delighted in reading aloud the latest bad poems sent to him by Sarah Binks.

more details of Sarah, and in 1947 Hiebert wrote her biography, "Sarah Binks, the Sweet Songstress of Saskatchewan," both a parody of literary pretensions and a masterpiece of comic satire. In 1948 Hiebert was awarded the Stephen Leacock Award for humour for his subject's rustic poetry and naive portrayal of life on the prairies in 1920s Saskatchewan.

According to Hiebert, in writing Sarah's biography he visited the literary outposts of Quagmire, Pelvis and Quorum, Saskatchewan as well as Vertigo, Manitoba. There he interviewed the people who inspired Sarah — people who would be legends in the west had they not been completely forgotten. Among them were Miss Rosalind Drool, Mathilda Schwartzenhacker, Ole the hired man and even Rover the dog. Hiebert gleaned other bits of information from Dr. Taj Mahal, who studied railway timetables in an attempt to better understand Sarah, and Mr. Justice Linseed, who wrote his own classic of prairie literature, "Eighty Years on the Bench."

Despite her massive and early success (barely an issue of the Horsebreeder's Gazette was published without at least one Binks poem) Sarah never forgot her roots, as illustrated in this deeply moving tribute to prairie farmers.

The farmer is monarch in high estate
Of his barn and his backhouse and byre,
And all the buildings behind the gate
Of his two-odd miles of barbed wire.

The most successful of Sarah's poems combined incongruity of idea and diction with an appeal to nostalgia. The idea that Steve would fall in love with the voice of neighbouring Mathilda sweetly calling a sow is both appealing and incongruous:

And oh, I think I'll hide again
For just a sight of you,
And hear your own sweet voice again
Call "Sooky, Sooky, Soo."

In "The Wedding Dress" Sarah combines a veiled reference to the shape of a pregnant bride with a nostalgic comment on catalogue-shopping:

On page two hundred and sixty three
Oh, there's the very dress for me...
Though after the wedding day we find
It's short in front and long behind,
And winds on heath
Get underneath
And rattle bones, and ribs, and teeth.

If Hiebert is to be believed, Sarah's accomplishments were legendary. She was the founder of the influential "geo-literary" school of Canadian verse, winner of Saskatchewan's highest poetic honour — the Wheat Pool Medal — for her epic "Up From the Magma and Back Again," and she was the creator of such heart-rending lyrics as:

I'm a genius, I'm a genius
What more can I desire,
I toot upon my little flute,
And twang upon my lyre;
I dabble in oil paint,
In cinnebar and ochre,
All night I am dissipated,
And play poker.

Biting down on a mint as she was taking her own temperature, [Binks] cracked the thermometer and swallowed the mercury.

Sarah's life came to a sad and untimely end when her love of mints and the debilitating effect of a fever combined to bring about her death. Biting down on a mint as she was taking her own temperature, she cracked the thermometer and swallowed the mercury. Sadly, had she not been using a horse thermometer she might have survived.

Hiebert was a regular guest on Peter Gzowski's CBC program "Morningside," and the biography of Sarah Binks is considered a Canadian classic. In 1995 "A Sarah Binks Songbook" written by Canadian composer John Greer and performed by soprano Helen Pridmore was presented for the first time, and in 2003 Sarah Binks was selected for the annual CBC Radio's Canada Reads competition.

Paul Hiebert died on 7 September 1987 and is buried in Carman, Manitoba. ✦

# 1872-1948

## FREDERICK PHILIP GREVE/GROVE

**F**elix Paul Greve was a minor early 20th century German poet, novelist, translator, and playwright before he became one of the most significant Canadian writers of the early twentieth century and a founder of the realist tradition in modern Canadian fiction.

Greve was born in 1872 in East Prussia to German parents who separated when he was a child. He was a philology student at Bonn University where he lived considerably beyond his means before leaving without graduating to write a book of poetry and a volume of verse drama. The same year they were published he began an affair with a married woman, with whom he lived on money fraudulently borrowed from a friend. In 1903 he was convicted of fraud and sentenced to a year in prison. Two years after his release he published his first major work, an intensely psychological novel about the growing disillusionment and decline of a German actress. Unable to live by his writing alone, Greve worked long hours as a translator. Despite his prodigious efforts, however, he was unable to pay his considerable debts. Facing a second prison term, he faked his suicide in 1909 and secretly emigrated to North America, where he changed his name to Frederick Philip Grove. It was not until the 1970s that it became known that the minor German writer who committed suicide in 1909 was Frederick

• Frederick Philip
Greve/Grove

Grove's realism is almost photographic and provides one of the most detailed and believable portraits of rural life in all of literature.

Philip Grove, one of the most respected writers in Canadian history.

Grove led an itinerant life in the United States before he obtained a job as a permit teacher in a Mennonite village near Winkler. After attending normal school he became principal of the intermediate school at Winkler. He then moved to Virden and in 1916 to Gladstone, where he was principal of a a number of area schools, one of which was a small rural school near Falmouth, northeast of Gladstone. It became the setting of his finest novels.

In 1921 Grove moved to Rapid City. Two years later he left teaching to devote himself to writing full time. His first Canadian book was published in 1922 and his second a year later. His first novel, *Settlers of the Marsh* (1925), established Grove's reputation as one of the founders of the prairie-realist school of Canadian fiction. The novel tells the tale of a man manipulated by forces he cannot control as he tries to wrest a living from the Manitoba marshlands. Grove's realism is almost photographic and provides a detailed and believable portrait of rural life.

By the time Grove left Manitoba in 1929 to become president and editor of Graphic Publishers in Ottawa he was one of the country's most respected writers of serious fiction. Two years before he died Grove published what was later determined to be a fictional autobiography, *In Search of Myself*. It won the Governor General's Award in 1946 for non-fiction.

The seventy-six year old author died of a stroke in 1948 and was buried beside his much loved daughter in the southwest corner of Rapid City's cemetery. Ironically, the identity he tried so hard to conceal and his strange life story now seem more memorable and engaging than his fiction. ✦

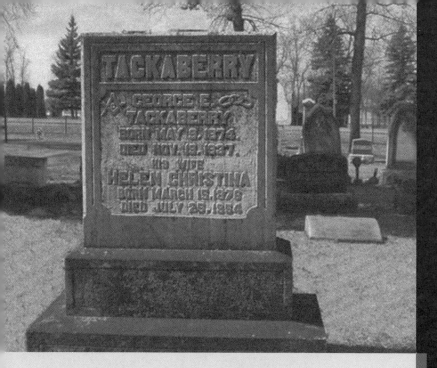

# 1874-1937

## GEORGE EDWIN TACKABERRY

Sometimes casual conversations over the back fence generate more than idle gossip. So it was early in the twentieth century when "Bad Joe Hall" was chatting with neighbour George Tackaberry.

Joseph Henry Hall was born in Staffordshire, England, in 1882 but raised in Manitoba. Hall was equal parts talent and toughness, known throughout Canada for his aggressive, hard hitting style. In 1905 he scored 33 goals in only 20 games, but also led the Manitoba Hockey League in penalty minutes. Despite his rough play, and suspension for punching a referee, Hall played on two Stanley Cup teams and lost in another final.

One hundred years ago it was no irony that one of hockey's greatest players was a European. Games between teams hitting an object with curved sticks have been played throughout history. Several Egyptian tombs depict a sport resembling field hockey, and in the 16th century the Galway Statutes in Ireland made reference to "the horlinge of the litill balle with hockie sticks or staves."According to hockey historian Stan Fischler the roots of hockey can be traced back 500 years to Great Britain, where field hockey was a popular summer sport. When the country's ponds and lakes froze in winter, it was not unusual for enthusiasts to play on ice. European immigrants brought various versions of hockey-

like games to North America, including the Scottish sport of shinty, the Irish sport of hurling and the field hockey played in England.

By 1905, however, hockey had undergone considerable change. Players like Bad Joe Hall had become as hard on their equipment as they were on their opponents. That was particularly true of their boots. This is where Hall's conversation with his shoemaker-neighbour George Tackaberry set the stage for a remarkable revolution in the manufacture of hockey skates.

The first skate was manufactured in 1863 when a Nova Scotia company manufactured a metal blade, invented fifteen years earlier in Philadelphia, that a skater could fasten to his boot with leather straps as he was about to take to the ice. The next significant technological advance occurred in the late nineteenth century when the Bauer family introduced a skate in which a blade assembly was permanently attached to a boot. The Bauer Supreme dominated the skate market until 1905, when the Canadian Cycle and Motor Company, better known as CCM, began manufacturing winter sports equipment, including their own brand of skates.

Tackaberry addressed Hall's need for a better skate with a combination of innovative design and meticulous handcrafting. After the shoemaker carefully measured Hall's feet the two men together designed a new boot, made out of kangaroo hide because of its resistance to moisture and stretching. They lowered the top of the boot nearly two inches and added a snuggly fitting reinforced heel and toe and a much improved arch support.

Hall was so enthusiastic about his skate that soon others experimented with the new design. Among the first were Lester Patrick of the New York Rangers and Art Ross of the Boston Bruins. Almost over night Tackaberry was swamped with orders, and the reputation of his high quality skate spread through locker rooms in arenas from coast to coast. Tacks quickly became the hockey world's most famous name in skates.

When George Tackaberry died in 1937 CCM acquired the Tackaberry trade name and his many innovations. Over the next thirty years the Tackaberry boot with its CCM Pro-Lite blade was worn by every scoring champion in the National Hockey League.

In his obituary notice the *Brandon Sun* rightly described Tackaberry as a man of ability and resourcefulness, an outstanding figure in the community. His accomplishments influenced a Toronto area life-style publication, the *Tackaberry Times*, to adopt his name as symbol of an era when trips to town were an event, neighbours depended on each other, and a frozen pond was a community's skating rink.

George Edwin Tackaberry was born in 1874 in Dresden, Ontario, where he apprenticed as a shoemaker before moving west to work in the Zinc Brothers shoe shop in Brandon. He is buried beside his wife Helen in the Brandon Cemetery. Bad Joe Hall was just thirty-six years old when he became a victim of the influenza epidemic which swept North America in 1919. He is buried in Mountain View Cemetery in Vancouver, British Columbia. He was inducted into the Hockey Hall of Fame in 1961. ✦

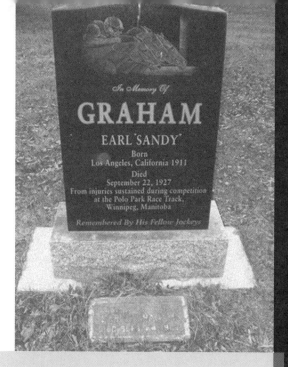

In Memory Of
# GRAHAM
### EARL 'SANDY'
Born
Los Angeles, California 1911
Died
September 22, 1927
From injuries sustained during competition
at the Polo Park Race Track,
Winnipeg, Manitoba

*Remembered By His Fellow Jockeys*

# 1911-1927

# EARL 'SANDY' GRAHAM

The author of *Seabiscuit: An American Legend* wrote that we have a tendency to remember what we would most like to forget, and forget what we would be best served to remember. Never has that been more true than when recounting the tragic death of a sixteen- year-old jockey, mortally wounded at Winnipeg's old Polo Park racetrack.

In 1927 Tommy Luther and Earl "Sandy" Graham were novice riders and best friends, and the two were scheduled to ride against each other on a pair of stablemates. Luther was originally given Vesper Lad, a plodding and uncoordinated colt, while Graham was to ride the much faster Irish Princess II. Just before the race the horses' trainer reversed the assignments. Minutes later, as Luther and Irish Princess crossed the finish line ahead of the pack, the jockey heard the crowd gasp. Turning to see what had happened, he saw Graham lying motionless on the ground. Vesper Lad had rammed the rail, throwing his rider to the track, where he had been trampled by the field.

While Luther dismounted and returned to the scales his friend lay crumpled in the homestretch dirt, his ribs and back shattered. Polo Park had no ambulance, and so Graham was carried to the jockey's

Polo Park had no ambulance, and so Graham was carried to the jockeys' room, where he was left on a saddle table, alone.

room, where he was left on a saddle table, alone. Although Luther begged track officials to take his friend to a hospital, they refused to do so until the day's racing was over.

The fact that riders were forbidden to help him sealed Graham's fate. Since his fellow jockeys were contracted to ride in upcoming races, leaving their room to attend to him would have been a career-ending decision.

Luther passed the hat to raise taxi fare, but because jockeys were denied a cut of purses and most lived in a state of virtual poverty, there was not enough. As a result, for the rest of the afternoon all Luther could do was sit beside his friend, dripping water into his mouth. By the time someone eventually drove Graham to the hospital it was too late. After lingering in pain for a few days, he died. Jockey fatalities were so common that his passing went virtually unnoticed.

Since Graham had neither savings nor insurance, and since his family was penniless, he was buried in a Winnipeg pauper's grave. Luther, meanwhile, despite being overwhelmed by grief, moved on to another venue. Over the next decade his career blossomed. He was rider of the year in 1927, and the following year he won 90 races in a 70-day stretch, topping his season by winning the Coffroth Handicap, then the world's richest race.

Throughout the 1930s Luther continued to ride horses like War Relic and the brilliant Time Supply, but he remained haunted by Graham's appalling treatment and unnecessary death. Luther was convinced that his life had been spared for a reason, and he believed that the reason was to improve the conditions under which jockeys worked, and often died.

In the late 1930s he and several other riders held a series of secret meetings to discuss the idea of forming a union. Racing stewards soon learned of the gatherings, and they summoned Luther to a meeting of their own. They accused him of starting a union and banned him from riding for a year, but Luther's idea took hold. Thanks to his efforts the Jockeys' Guild survived, and today riders have insurance, much better pay, improved working conditions and better health care.

After he left racing to train horses Luther remained deeply hurt by the fact that few of his contemporaries remembered the Guild's origins. He spent his last years devoted to ensuring that modern jockeys knew that the benefits they enjoyed came at the price of Sandy Graham's life. The Guild, he said, was not born at an American racetrack. "It started in Canada, when that boy fell."

The story of the death of Sandy Graham has been immortalized in a song recently released by Maine-born Texas balladeer Slaid Cleaves. His songs are superbly crafted stories drawn from real life, and he wrote about Luther after reading a few paragraphs about him in *Seabiscuit*.

Well it's Winnipeg and it's raining
But the track's not looking bad.
They gave me Irish Princess
Sandy rode on Vesper Lad.
We were flying down the backstretch
My horse was running proud
I pulled ahead of Sandy
When a roar came from the crowd.

I crouched as Irish Princess
Thundered across the line
And then I stood and turned around
To see that friend of mine
Vesper Lad was standing still.
There must have been a fall

And in the mud lay Sandy
Looking lifeless as a doll.

It was poor old Mother Harris
From the boarding house in town
Who paid for the little casket
And laid him in the ground

I sent a couple of dollars
It was all that I could save
She drew me a little picture
Of the lonely rider's grave.
I've kept it in my bedroom drawer
All these sixty years.
I still see that crumpled body now
But I'm too old for tears.
My name is Tommy Luther…

Polo Park racetrack was opened in 1925 on Portage Avenue at St. James Street. It was closed thirty years later to make way for construction of the Polo Park Shopping Centre. In 2003 a large headstone and plaque were erected over Sandy Graham's grave in the Brookside Cemetery. ✦

# 1938-1997

## ROBERT HAROLD "BULLDOG" BROWN

"Bulldog"

ROBERT H. BROWN
OCTOBER 25, 1938
FEBRUARY 5, 1997

"Bulldog" Brown was not like other wrestlers with gimmicky names and bulging physiques. He shunned shiny robes and fancy accessories in favour of simple blue trunks and a flat-top haircut. At 240 pounds and well under six feet tall he was a brawler with at best average skill. Yet this western Manitoba native became wrestling's most hated villain, a performer who gave no quarter and asked for none.

Robert Harold Brown was born in Shoal Lake on October 25th, 1938, although he spent his formative years in Winnipeg. From beginning to end of his thirty-three year career he was associated with the biggest names in wrestling. As a novice he trained with Verne Gagne and Bronko Nagurski, numbering among tag-team partners the likes of Gene Kiniski and that all-time wrestling icon, Andre the Giant.

Brown entered this "theatre of the absurd" in the early 1960s. He was equal measures a bully and smart-alec, and he reveled in the performance aspect of wrestling. More often than not fans were unwitting participants. In one city a fan hated Bulldog so much that, whenever he was introduced and began his walk from the dressing room to the ring, the screaming woman would stalk him, armed with an ice-filled cup of Coca-Cola and shouting "You dirty, no good, stinking s.o.b." As she let fly her drink she invariably said the same thing: "I hope you get killed tonight."

Brown always knew it was coming, and would often slow down so that she could play her part. Each week his response was the same. "You fat, toothless, ugly..." he would shout, wiping the soft drink from his eyes. When the screaming reached its peak he would simply nod to his tormentor and enter the ring.

Although Brown was always the bad guy, he had a large and enthusiastic fan base. One of the most dedicated was asked why he supported the Bulldog. He answered by describing a match he attended in Kansas City. When Brown entered the arena "I started cheering, but a young man of about twelve sitting next to me started booing. The young man leaned over and said 'Bulldog's a bad guy. Why are you cheering for him?' Just then Bulldog came around to our side of the ring and hopped onto the apron. The young man stood up and gave him the finger, yelling 'Bulldog, you suck!' Brown pulled up a 'loogie' from the deepest part of his lungs and spit it right between the eyes of that young man. I leaned over and said 'Now you know why I cheer for the bad guy.'"

Sometimes the action, usually by mistake, was all too real. On one occasion Brown's opponent actually made contact with him when the Bulldog was pretending to

Although Brown was always the bad guy, he had a large and enthusiastic fan base.

knee him in the mid-section. The contact threw Brown off balance, and he did two complete revolutions before falling on his opponent. The two crashed heads, ending the fight and nearly knocking each other out.

Often the best matches of the night were in the dressing rooms. At every venue there were always wrestlers who could not stop their taunting, and fights of the real kind were common. According to one of Brown's partners, "If the other guys liked 'em they'd step in. If not they'd just watch and hope somebody got hurt." Fans, however, posed a far more serious threat of injury to wrestlers. Folding chairs were a particular menace. A record of some sort was set during a match in Winnipeg, when 103 landed in the ring.

Television captured it all. Some ringside fans were seen so often that they became celebrities in their own right. Two of the most recognized were Mertie and Gertie Hite. The seventy-five year-old twin sisters invariably occupied ringside seats, where, dressed exactly alike, they usually sat calmly, the picture of rectitude. When some mysterious force moved

> To knowledgeable wrestling fans Brown had a heart of gold and was considered a truly nice person in a violent business. His good heart, however, was something he was careful to keep hidden.

within them, however, they would leap to their feet and race screaming to the edge of the ring, where they would pound wildly on the canvas and curse like drunken sailors.

To knowledgeable wrestling fans Brown had a heart of gold and was considered a truly nice person in a violent business. His good heart, however, was something he was careful to keep hidden. An exception occurred during a training session when an aspiring wrestler was roughed up badly. When the session ended he sat alone, elbows bloody from practising falls. All the other wrestlers had left, except for Brown. The Bulldog looked around to make sure that they were alone, then he helped the novice clean up his elbows and urged him to get some antiseptic cream on them so that they would not get infected.

One of Brown's trademarks was his misuse of the English language. For one road trip his brother made him headcheese sandwiches. When he could no longer tolerate the comments of his travelling companions, Brown shouted in irritation "Don't you know that headcheese is a delicatessen!" On another occasion Brown was fighting on a Manitoba Indian reserve. He drew thunderous jeers when during the introductions he commented on all the great "abortional" Indians in attendance.

Brown retired from the ring in 1996 after suffering a massive heart attack. He was working as a cashier at a valet parking lot of the Flamingo floating casino in Kansas City, Missouri when he died a year later, aged fifty-nine.

During a six-man tag team event going on the day Brown died, two of his friends were standing on the ring apron side by side. Superstar Bill Dundee turned to his opponent and asked him if he had heard that the Bulldog had just died. The two then started reminiscing, while the match was going on, oblivious both to what was happening in the ring and to the screams of fans.

A long time friend of Brown took up a collection at the Kansas City racetrack to do something special for his former tag-team partner. The response was overwhelming. "We were going to send flowers. But we got enough to pay for his gravestone up in Winnipeg. I thought it was nice that people remembered him so kindly after all these years."

Robert Harold Bulldog Brown died on February 5th, 1997 and is buried in Winnipeg's Brookside Cemetery. ✦

WITHOUT A DOUBT MANITOBA HAS BEEN THE SCENE OF SOME
SENSATIONAL CRIMES. Lord Gordon Gordon was a swindler of epic proportion,
and one of the only men to bilk the famous American entrepreneur Jay Gould out
of a few of his many millions. The story of Lawrence Lees is not about money,
but of a man who died because he did his job too well. Like Gordon Gordon, John
Machray was a swindler. The nephew of an archbishop stole millions and in the
process nearly bankrupt a university and the province's Anglican Church. If it were
not for its fatal conclusion the bicycle hold-up of Henry Roch would read like a
modern farce. The fate that befell the Sitar family, however, was all tragedy, made
worse because the family died at the hands of one of their own. The chapter
concludes with a description of a scandal that brought down a government and
nearly sent a provincial premier to jail.

# CHAPTER 4

# crime

# 1935

# BENITO MURDERS

IN LOVING MEMORY OF
WILLIAM WAINWRIGHT
BORN APR. 4, 1880
DIED OCT. 5, 1935.
DIED WHILE
PERFORMING HIS DUTY

In the fall of 1935 western Canadians were at the same time shocked and captivated by a series of vicious crimes that, in just five days, involved a massive man-hunt over three provinces, the death of three fugitives, and tragically the murder of four police officers. Ironically, the crimes were committed by members of a religious order committed to non-violence.

The Doukhobors were a Christian sect which in the eighteenth century rejected secular government, church ritual, the Bible and the divinity of Jesus. Because of these beliefs they faced increasing prosecution in their Russian homeland and, beginning in 1899, most fled to Canada, where the government provided them with three reserves. Ottawa also enacted a "Hamlet Clause" so they could live communally, since the Doukhobors did not believe in individual land ownership.

What they did believe in was pacifism and non-violence. So strong was their commitment to both that most Doukhobors accepted that from the moment a member participated in an act of violence, he or she ceased to be a Doukhobor. This made it hard to understand the carnage that began in Benito, Manitoba, a small town near the Saskatchewan border.

Sometime after midnight on Friday, October 4th, town constable William Wainwright and Constable John Shaw from the Royal Canadian Mounted Police detachment in Swan River questioned three men who were seen in the vicinity of a recent attempted burglary. The police identified them as twenty-one year-old John Kalmakoff, twenty year-old Joseph Posnikoff, and Peter Woiken, eighteen. All were sons of Saskatchewan Doukhobors. The trio and their car were searched, but since no weapons were found, they were allowed to leave.

After further discussion, however, Wainwright and Shaw decided that the men might be the fugitives wanted for a robbery in Pelly, Saskatchewan, a town situated 26 kilometres west of Benito. Around 4:00 am they again located the three. This time they were ordered out of their car and, without being searched, placed in the rear of the unmarked police cruiser.

Shortly after Shaw and his passengers reached the highway to Pelly one of the Doukhobors suddenly slashed Wainwright's neck and head with a knife. The three then wrestled Wainwright's gun from him and one of them used it to shoot the wounded officer in the eye. A second drew his own pistol and shot Shaw several times in the head. When the prisoners climbed out of the car, which had crashed into a ditch, they stripped the policemen of their identification and threw their bodies into a slough.

The two officers were found Monday morning by a local farmer, but by the time a man-hunt was organized the fugitives were already in Alberta. When they stopped for gas eleven miles east of Canmore the attendant's wife recognized the missing police car by its Manitoba licence plate and notified the Canmore RCMP, who in turn alerted the Banff detachment.

In Banff Sergeant Thomas Wallace and another off-duty policeman immediately headed east with two uniformed officers, one of whom was Constable George Harrison. On the same highway, but miles ahead of the four pursuers, the fugitives stopped a car and robbed its occupants of their valuables and $10.00 in cash. Then for some reason they followed the very vehicle they had just stopped.

When Wallace and Harrison were less than ten feet away two shots ripped through its windshield, hitting Harrison in the throat and Wallace in the chest.

Four miles east of Banff National Park the robbery victims flagged down the on-coming car driven by the four policemen, and told the officers about the men in the car behind them. Wallace and Harrison immediately got out of their car and walked towards the now parked getaway vehicle. When they were less than ten feet away two shots ripped through its windshield, hitting Harrison in the throat and Wallace in the chest.

Before collapsing both men managed to fire at their assailants, but as a second police car drove up the three Doukhobors jumped out of their vehicle and slipped into bush beside the highway. Within minutes, however, one of the pursing officers spotted something moving at the edge of the thick brush and opened fire, hitting Posnikoff in the head and killing him instantly.

Within hours outraged volunteers and police officers from neighbouring detachments flooded into the area. Highways were closed, cars were checked, and for the first time in the history of the Royal Canadian Mounted Police, a police dog was brought in to participate in a search conducted under gunfire. Although the night was cold and searchers were plagued by a combination of rain, hail and snow, the dog quickly picked up the trail of the wanted men.

Around 10:30 the next morning one of the search groups was fired at by someone hiding in the bush. Among the searchers was a game warden, who immediately returned fire, hitting Woiken. The warden then noticed the glint of another rifle barrel, and opened fire a second time, striking Kalmakoff. Although the two fugitives were transported to Banff Mineral Springs Hospital, both died shortly after being admitted.

The two police officers wounded in the initial exchange of gunfire were taken first to a hospital in Canmore and then to Calgary, where both succumbed to their injuries. A few days later thousands lined Calgary streets as the body of Wallace was taken to Calgary's Union Cemetery, and that of Harrison to Banff. In one of the most touching scenes of the day, Harrison's black charger walked behind its owner's hearse, the slain officer's boots reversed in the stirrups.

Kalmakoff's body was taken home by family members and buried in an unmarked grave in a Saskatchewan field. The bodies of Posnikoff and Woiken were never claimed by their families. Because of the anger of Banff and Canmore residents, they were not buried in either community. Instead, their remains were taken to Morley, Alberta, where they were interred in unmarked graves adjacent to the Wesley Cemetery.

Constable William Wainwright was laid to rest in Benito's cemetery, while Constable John George Shaw was buried in Birchwood Cemetery in Swan River. ✦

# LORD GORDON
# GORDON

As Huck Finn and his companion Jim drifted down the Mississippi, deep in discussion, they were joined by two swindlers who claimed to be a king and a duke. Jim doubted their credentials and suspected that the smelly drunkards were in truth only rapscallions. Huck agreed but noted that royalty "is mostly rapscallions." Of no one in the history of Canada was this more true than Manitoba's own Lord Gordon Gordon.

Gordon Gordon first appeared in England in 1868 variously claiming to be a ward in Chancery of the Earl of Glencairn, a cousin of the late Marquis of Hastings, a relative of the Duke of Hamilton, and an intimate friend of the Prince of Wales. Relying on these fictions a prominent firm of Scottish jewelers sold him thousands of pounds worth of jewelry on credit, and a well known solicitor personally guaranteed a number of Gordon Gordon's largest purchases. After running up enormous debts all over Great Britain, the smooth talking Scot disappeared for a year and a half before surfacing in Minneapolis, Minnesota in 1871. There he registered at a local hotel as Lord Gordon Gordon, and in casual conversation let it be known that he was interested in buying land on which he planned to settle some of his Scottish folk.

• Lord Gordon
Gordon

His comments attracted the attention of Northern Pacific Railway officials, and Gordon Gordon was asked to join a hunting party about to depart for the American west. By the time the caravan left it consisted of forty horses, twelve men to pitch tents, a French cook, waiters outfitted in linen aprons and silk gloves, a covered wagon containing weapons for deer hunting and a second equipped with

fishing tackle, and for Gordon Gordon's personal use two tents, a valet, a secretary and fourteen changes of clothes. In the end the rail company spent more than forty thousand dollars courting a man who invested not a penny in either its land or its stock.

Shortly after returning from his western excursion Gordon Gordon left Minneapolis for New York with a number of letters of introduction, including one addressed to Horace Greeley, famous for his slogan "Go West, Young Man." Gordon lived quietly for a couple of months before he met Jay Gould. Gould had acquired a fortune through unscrupulous business deals and insider trading, and when Gordon Gordon arrived in New York the famous American robber baron was engaged in a fight for control of the Erie Railroad Company.

By 1872 a majority of shares in the railroad were held by British investors trying to oust Gould from the presidency of the Erie. Presenting himself as a major shareholder of the rail company, Lord Gordon Gordon seemed like the answer to the businessman's prayers. Gould was told that the Scot owned $30,000,000 of Erie stock personally and had control of an additional $20,000,000 belonging to his English associates. Gould swallowed the whole line. Two weeks after meeting Gordon Gordon the railroader transferred to his new friend over two thousand shares in Erie and its associated companies, together with nearly $200,000 in cash.

Because of his checkered past and manner of death Headingley church elders refused to bury the infamous Scot in their local graveyard.

Gordon Gordon immediately sold five thousand shares of the Oil Creek and Allegheny River Railroad. The sale attracted the attention of Gould, who demanded that the Scotsman return his money and securities. When his one-time saviour kept $150,000 of the cash, Gould had him arrested.

At trial Gordon Gordon was asked about his relatives and associates. Gould promptly cabled those named and soon learned that they had never heard of the alleged Scottish lord. When Gordon Gordon learned about the inquiries he departed for Montreal, and from there he made his way to Winnipeg.

For the next two years Gordon Gordon rented a room in Headingley, until he was arrested. Although the thirty-year-old fugitive gave up without protest, he asked permission to put on a warmer coat for the trip east. Immediately on entering his room he took a pistol from his night stand and, according to a contemporary account, shot himself like a gentleman.

Although no one knows for certain the true identity of this man, known variously as Hamilton, Glencairn, George Hubert Gordon and Lord Gordon Gordon, most believe that he was part of a family of international smugglers who operated from the Isle of Jersey.

Because of his checkered past and manner of death Headingley church elders refused to bury the infamous Scot in their local graveyard. Although laid to rest just outside the community's burial ground, Manitoba's most infamous scoundrel had the last laugh. As Headingley expanded and more and more of the community's residents died, the cemetery was enlarged, and when its boundary fence was moved the con man's grave was brought within consecrated grounds.

Lord Gordon Gordon is buried in the north-east corner of the Headingley cemetery. ✦

# 1877-1932

## LAWRENCE LEES

There was a buzz of anticipation in Rossburn, Manitoba on June 3rd, 1932. Everyone knew everyone else and most were looking forward to the marriage of a popular local girl to a well known Clear Lake game warden. Excitement, however, was short-lived. A little over a month later Lawrence Lees was to die by an assassin's bullet, leaving his widow, Myrtez Burnette, badly wounded and maimed for life.

In the 1920s the growing popularity of Clear Lake as a summer resort posed a serious threat to area wildlife, and reports by local forest rangers increasingly referred to declining numbers of game animals. In response, the federal government decided to transform Riding Mountain National Park into a game reserve. No longer would it issue hunting licences, and forest rangers were reclassified as wardens, responsible for enforcing the new regulations.

The changes created considerable resentment in the Rossburn area, and many residents were not prepared to stop shooting game within the confines of the park. Their decision to continue hunting eventually led to a number of violent confrontations between poachers and wardens.

Lees was thirty-two years old when he immigrated to Canada from England in 1909. After World War I ended he joined the Dominion Forest Service and was posted to several Manitoba stations before being transferred to Deep Lake Ranger Station fourteen miles north of Rossburn. Lees quickly earned a community reputation for both his efficiency and strict enforcement of hunting regulations.

During the afternoon of July 13th the Lees were at home when they heard shooting in the park, a not unusual occurrence. Lawrence suspected that poachers were at work and immediately left his bride of five weeks to investigate. When he returned a few hours later he said nothing of the incident.

Shortly before 10:00 pm a tall man dressed in blue overalls and a grey sweater crept through the dense bush surrounding the Lees's cabin, crouching behind a picket fence on the north side, approximately 100 feet from an open kitchen window. Seconds after Lees and his wife sat down for a late supper the assassin fired his first shot. The bullet struck the game warden above his left collar bone and severed his spinal cord, killing him instantly.

As soon as Myrtez realized what had happened she ran to her husband's office and grabbed his revolver. When she got back to the kitchen she threw open the rear door and fired a shot at the outline of someone bent behind her garden fence. As the diminutive widow retreated into the

**Seconds after Lees and his wife sat down for a late supper the assassin fired his first shot.**

cottage the killer stood and walked around the structure, looking through one window after another until he found her in the office.

In a voice Myrtez recognized but could not quite place, the man told the panicked woman that he had "damned good reasons for shooting your husband. He should have been shot long ago." The killer then told her that if she gave him the gun Lawrence had seized that afternoon she would not be harmed.

Myrtez ignored the demand and grabbed the cabin's phone, a land-line connecting the isolated cottage to the main game warden office. She only managed to shout "Lawrence has been shot" before a bullet ripped through the back of her neck, shattering her jaw and tearing a two-inch hole out of her cheek.

As Mrs. Lees lay in a growing pool of her own blood the assassin took the screen off the kitchen window and entered the house. After searching Lawrence's pockets he moved to the office. There he rifled through the warden's desk, ignoring a small quantity of money. He then tore from Lees's diary three pages of notes made over the previous days, grabbed the revolver lying on the floor, and walked out.

The panicked call of Mrs. Lees brought an immediate response. Law enforcement officials throughout the district rushed to the cabin, where an operational base was quickly established. The ensuing search drew RCMP constables from Russell, Dauphin, Minnedosa and Clear Lake, as well as dozens of civilian searchers.

It was almost twenty-four hours later before the two area doctors called to the scene felt that Myrtez was stable enough to be moved to a hospital. Officials used the car of a *Winnipeg Tribune* reporter to transport her to Shoal Lake, where she started a hospital stay which was to last the rest of the year.

The hunt for Lees's killer lasted a week. Although the RCMP was convinced that the shooter lived in the

**The hunt for Lees's killer lasted a week. The murder remains unsolved.**

area, the dead warden's mostly east European neighbours remained silent, denying even having heard the large-bore discharges that killed Lees and injured his wife. The murder remains unsolved.

Lawrence Lees was buried in his family's plot in Neepawa. After suffering through a series of operations and six months of convalescence Mrytez moved to Winnipeg, where she joined the *Free Press Prairie Farmer*. She passed away on 29 June 1991 and is buried in Winnipeg's Brookside cemetery. ✦

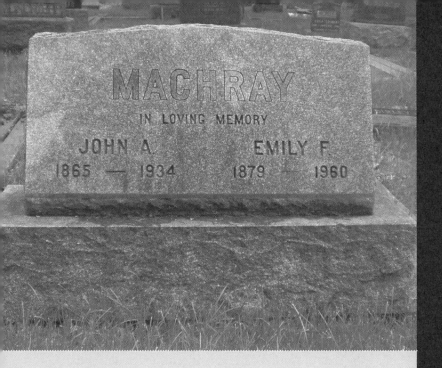

# 1865-1933

## JOHN ALEXANDER MACHRAY

He seemed to have it all. He was the nephew of an archbishop, the son-in-law of one of Manitoba's wealthiest men, a senior partner in a prestigious law firm, and the person responsible for investing moneys of the Anglican church and the province's largest university. Yet when he died, instead of being surrounded by loving family and friends, he lay in a prison hospital, convicted of what is believed to be the largest embezzlement in Manitoba's history.

Although John Alexander Machray is now forgotten, in the first three decades of the twentieth century he was one of Winnipeg's most prominent citizens. Trusted by clients and colleagues, deeply committed to a handful of charitable organizations, he was well connected both socially and financially. His uncle was the archbishop of Rupertsland and his wife the daughter of brewery magnate E. L. Drewry.

For the first twenty years of his life Machray lived in the household of his influential and domineering uncle, often traveling as his secretary, attending church meetings and gaining an intimate knowledge of the archdiocese, and its finances.

In 1884 Machray graduated from the University of Manitoba with an honours degree and silver medal. He then attended Cambridge, one of England's most famous universities, before returning to Winnipeg to practise law with Heber Archibald.

Archibald was his uncle's legal advisor and closest friend, and it was his job to manage the trust funds of the Rupertsland archdiocese. When Archibald retired in 1905 control of his law firm passed to Machray, who also took over as investment officer for the region's Anglican church. Two years later he became legal counsel to the archdiocese and at the same won a bid to manage the University of Manitoba's endowment funds.

When Machray became involved with the university it held just under half a million dollars in a variety of investments. Within twenty years that amount had more than doubled, largely because of donations made by large corporations and wealthy benefactors. For instance, the Rockefeller Foundation donated half a million dollars to the university to help it establish a medical faculty, and the Carnegie Foundation gave nearly $100,000 to set up a faculty pension fund. John Machray was responsible for managing these monies, along with those of the Anglican church and a number of private investors, including retired pastors and his mentor, Heber Archibald.

In 1907 Winnipeg was a city of opportunity. Its population was increasing dramatically between 1906 and 1916, and housing was in short supply. Although Machray had no money of his own, he was caught up in the excitement of the times. Using church and university funds, he entered into numerous partnerships to buy and develop real estate, and he provided the seed money to establish several new businesses.

When Winnipeg's real estate bubble burst, shortly before the start of World War I, Machray owned a substantial amount of non-performing real estate worth substantially less than what he had paid. In short, Machray was bankrupt. Instead of admitting his mismanagement to church and university officials, however, he decided to conceal his financial plight and hang on to his holdings, making tax and loan payments out of their trust funds, in the vain hope that land values would recover.

During the 1920s Machray's financial position worsened, and he began taking even more ill-considered risks, moving trust moneys from the security of bonds into much more speculative investments, none of which paid off. In mid-1932 an independent auditor examined the lawyer's various accounts and quickly determined that his law firm had spent nearly $1,000,000 of university money. The school's board of governors promptly demanded that he re-pay the missing funds, and when he could not, he was charged with theft and arrested.

A month later Machray pleaded guilty to stealing $500,000 from the University of Manitoba and another $60,000 from Archibald. According to his lawyer, none of the missing funds had been used by Machray for his own benefit. His sole aim had been maintaining underperforming assets until he earned enough money to re-pay the amount he had misappropriated.

On 22 September 1932 Winnipeg police magistrate R. M. Noble sentenced his close friend to seven years in prison, the maximum sentence allowed by law, and a week later the provincial government established a royal commission to investigate the embezzlement.

It sat for fifty-four days and heard more than forty witnesses before announcing that Machray had stolen just under $2,000,000, the equivalent of more than $12,000,000 in today's funds. From the money taken $800,000 was paid to clients as interest on investments which did not exist, and $300,000 was used by Machray personally, a finding that refuted the suggestion made at trial that he did not benefit from mismanagement of the monies entrusted to him.

In early November 1932, Machray appeared before the royal commission. His cancer had progressed to the point

Like so many of his parishioners, he too had lost everything, including his savings and his home. Nonetheless, the Church of England brought no charges against the man who had betrayed it.

that he had to be carried from the prison hospital to an office on the penitentiary's second floor. He testified while lying in a cot, a truly pathetic figure and mere shadow of the man he had once been.

An almost equally pathetic figure was that of Samuel Pritchard Matheson, successor to Robert Machray as Anglican primate of Canada. Like so many of his parishioners, he too had lost everything, including his savings and his home. Nonetheless, the Church of England brought no charges against the man who had betrayed it.

John Alexander Machray died in Stony Mountain Penitentiary on 6 October 1933. He is buried in Winnipeg's St. John's Cathedral Cemetery beside his wife Emily. ✦

# 1891-1916

## HENRY ROCH

À LA MÉMOIRE
DE
NOTRE CHÈRE FRÈRE
HENRI ROCK
DU CHATELARD SUISSE
MORT D'UN ASSASSINAT
A HAYWOOD
LE 14 OCT. 1916
A L'ÂGE DE 25 ANS
Priens pour lui

R.I.P.

**M**anitoba's last recorded armed robbery of a horse and buggy involved a bicycle pursuit, an ambush, voices from God and the shotgun murder of a St. Claude man.

When Henry Roch headed his rig and team up the lane of the Robidoux farm on the evening of 13 October 1916 he had been selling household medicines and spices door-to-door for five days. As was the custom, he was asked to spend the night. Absent from the home was the Robidoux's nineteen-year-old son. Because he got home late, Oscar slept downstairs on a couch in the family parlour. He saw Roch for the first time the next morning as the pedlar sat on his wagon selling patent medicines to a group of hired men. The roll of bills he put in his pocket immediately attracted Robidoux's attention, and ten minutes after Roch headed out Oscar followed, peddling his bicycle as fast as he could with his father's shotgun slung over his shoulder.

Within minutes of leaving the Robidoux farm Roch stopped to sell some medicines to Louis Picod. As Picod watched Roch head back down his lane to the highway he noticed a man riding by on a bicycle. According to later testimony, after passing Roch, Oscar Robidoux had just enough time to hide in bushes bordering the highway. As the unsuspecting pedlar drove past Robidoux jumped out to fire the first of two shots. Although the blast hit Roch in the neck, he managed to get off his wagon and start running away from his assailant. Robidoux's second shot, however, shattered Roch's spine, killing him instantly. When his body was discovered later that day he was half-standing in the bushes in which he had sought refuge.

Within hours Oscar Robidoux made his way from St. Claude to Winnipeg, where he bought a train ticket to Montreal. By the time his train pulled into Ottawa, however, an inquest had already been held at St. Claude and a warrant issued for his arrest. Twenty-eight hours after it was signed Robidoux was arrested and in November 1916 a grand jury brought in a true bill formally charging him with Roch's murder. Within a week the young St. Claude farm hand began displaying for the first time symptoms of the mental instability which became his defence. Because the three Winnipeg 'alienists' who examined him were unsure whether he was sane, Robidoux's trial was postponed and a special jury empaneled to determine whether he was fit to stand trial. It heard two conflicting stories. One was advanced by the doctors who examined him. They testified that, although Robidoux knew the difference between right and wrong, he genuinely believed that he had been directed by the voice of God to murder Roch. The other story, advanced by friends and neighbours of the accused, denied that Robidoux had ever acted strangely or had spoken of hearing voices.

Robidoux's first trial got underway on 19 June 1917. It ended the next day when a juror asked to be excused because he was feeling ill. The entire panel was dismissed and within hours a new jury sworn. After hearing fifty witnesses it too was dismissed. While all twelve jurors agreed that Robidoux had murdered Roch, two were adamant that he was insane when he did so. A week later a third jury started hearing evidence, although this time the issue was not whether Robidoux was guilty of murder but whether he was sane when the murder took place.

On 12 July 1917 Oscar Robidoux made his final court appearance. Throughout a week of testimony from sixty witnesses he had paid little attention to what was going on around him, and when asked to stand to hear the jury's verdict, he did so with indifference. Only when told that on the 17th of October "between the hours of 7 o'clock in the morning and 12 noon, you shall be hanged by the neck until you are dead" did he show any emotion.

In the end Oscar Robidoux did not hang. Two weeks before he was to be executed his sentence was commuted. Roch is interred with other members of his family in the old cemetery in Notre Dame des Lourdes. ✦

# 1932

# THE SITAR FAMILY MASSACRE

SITAR

IN LOVING MEMORY OF OUR
FATHER · MOTHER
MARTIN · JOSEPHINE
DIED 1932 · DIED 1932

WALTER
JAN 29 1932
AGE 11 YEARS

PAUL
JAN 29 1932
AGE 4 YEARS

BERT
JAN 29 1932
AGE 10 YEARS

**T**om Hreczkosy had been working for his uncle for a year and a half when the devil told him to take an axe and kill the farmer and his family. For a month Hreczkosy fought against what he knew was wrong, but early in the morning of 29 January 1932 he gave in.

His first victim was Martin Sitar, already dressed and getting ready to start a day of chores. Once he was dispatched, Hreczkosy killed his aunt and quietly entered the rooms of his five cousins. When he was done he had become the most prolific mass murderer in Manitoba history.

Hreczkosy was twenty-five when he arrived from Poland. After working at odd jobs in Winnipeg and Ontario he ended up on the Sitar farm just west of Elma, a small farming community about thirty miles north-east of Winnipeg. He enjoyed working alongside his uncle and cousins, at least until shortly before Christmas 1931, when he had his first visit from Satan.

The devil appeared in conventional form, with hoofs and horns, accompanied by a buzzing black fly, which did the actual talking. It told him to murder the Sitars, and when he was done, to burn their house with their bodies in it. As Hreczkosy was later to confess, from that visit onward "the devil was in my heart."

The first indication that something was wrong was the smell of smoke wafting from the Sitar yard across the road to the farmhouse of Mike Kachur. He rushed to the Sitar's farmhouse, where he found the family's small story-and-a-half home in flames. When finally able to break down the door leading to the kitchen, Kachur stumbled onto the bodies of Martin and Josephine, the latter still barely alive.

Just as he got the Sitars outside Kachur's father arrived. The two immediately re-entered the burning house and in a matter of seconds located seven year-old Jennie and four year-old Paul, and carried them away from the fire. The Kachurs were about to enter the house again when they heard groans from what little of the building had not already collapsed. As they stood listening the second story suddenly crumbled into the flames billowing up from the first floor, and the two saw the body of an adult tumble into the conflagration.

More horrifying to the Kachurs than the sight of the Sitars' terribly burned bodies were the gaping wounds in

> More horrifying to the Kachurs than the sight of the Sitars' terribly burned bodies were the gaping wounds in their heads.

their heads. Yet amazingly, Paul Sitar was still alive. In a vain attempt to save his life area farmers fought through a blizzard to get a horse-drawn sleigh to the farm, and then north to a Canadian National Railway car waiting to rush the injured boy to Winnipeg. When the youngest of the Sitars finally arrived at the St. Boniface hospital he lived only long enough to moan "Oh, Tom, what are you doing to me?"

As soon as officials finished searching through the ruins of the destroyed farmhouse they realized that Hreczkosy was unaccounted for, and a massive manhunt was launched. For the next five days police officers and volunteers searched across the Canadian prairies and into the northern United States. Ironically, when Hreczkosy was found he was sitting beside railway tracks a few kilometres from the Sitar's farm, weak from the cold and lack of food.

During a brief preliminary inquiry held to determine whether he was fit to stand trial a letter Hreczkosy wrote to his brother was read into the record. In it the killer said that "I don't know myself what came to my head that I killed the whole family of Macko Sitar. I worked for Macko for a year and a half and it was good for me. And now some evil befell me and I can not figure out what led me to it, so I killed a whole family with an axe."

The story of the Sitar massacre was not the only report of violence published by Manitoba newspapers in the first week of February 1932. The Elma tragedy shared space with a discussion of the three hangings to be carried out on successive days that week, and stories about the manhunt for Albert Johnson, Canada's infamous Mad Trapper.

Hreczkosy went to trial a month after he was taken into custody. Following conclusion of two days of testimony his jury spent four hours deliberating before they asked for the legal definition of insanity. An hour later they announced that they were deadlocked. Mr. Justice John Adamson refused to call a mistrial and sent them back to resume deliberations. The next morning the jury was unanimous and, despite lingering questions about his sanity, Hreczkosy was convicted of the Sitar murders and sentenced to hang.

The day before he was to be executed the federal government commuted Hreczkosy's sentence to life imprisonment,

> The next morning the jury was unanimous and, despite lingering questions about his sanity, Hreczkosy was convicted of the Sitar murders and sentenced to hang.

largely because the report submitted to the Department of Justice by the superintendent of the Selkirk Mental Hospital left little doubt that Hreczkosky was insane when he became one of Canada's largest mass murderers.

The Sitar family is buried in the Stony Hill cemetery on the original site of Elma's St. Ludwiga Polish National Church. At the time of their deaths Martin and Josephine were both fifty-five, Frank was twenty, Walter eleven, Bert ten, Jennie seven and Paul was four.

In a twist of irony, the cemetery in which the seven Sitars are buried is located just yards from the remains of the fire ravaged house in which they died.

The Sitar's large headstone contains no reference to the horrific events of Friday, January 29th, 1931. ◆

# 1858-1924

## GEORGE ROBSON COLDWELL

At noon on the last Thursday in January 1924 one of the best known and highly regarded men in western Canada died at his home in Brandon. He was described by the *Brandon Sun* as the city's most outstanding figure, and in a token of bipartisan respect rarely seen, the Manitoba legislature adjourned in his honour. To allow citizens to pay personal tribute his body lay in state for three hours, and the city bell tolled at seven second intervals as the cortege moved solemnly from St. Matthew's Church to the Brandon cemetery. His funeral was attended by a Who's Who of prominent Manitobans, and it was said of him that nowhere in the province was there a more honest man. No one mentioned that less than ten years earlier this paragon of virtue had come within three jury votes of being convicted of the largest political fraud in the history of the province.

In those and the eight years which
followed his government transformed
the face of the province with a series of
large public works projects, including
construction of dozens of buildings and
hundreds of miles of roads.

George Robson Coldwell was born in Canada West, as
Ontario was known in 1858. He earned a Bachelor of Arts
degree from Toronto's Trinity College before becoming a
law student, and in 1882 was called to the bar of Manitoba.
He practised briefly in Winnipeg before moving to Brandon
where, for the next twelve years, he worked with Thomas
Mayne Daly, the city's first mayor and country's first juvenile court judge.

By 1907 Coldwell had been for twenty years one of the
most prominent and influential members of Brandon's city
council. Few were surprised when the province's premier
asked him to take the cabinet seat previously occupied by the
recently deceased member for Brandon City. On November
14th Coldwell entered the government of Rodmond Roblin,
as Provincial Secretary and Municipal Commissioner. Four
months later he resigned as Provincial Secretary to become
the province's first Minister of Education.

When Coldwell entered his cabinet Roblin had been
premier for six years. In those and the eight years which
followed his government transformed the face of the province with a series of large public works projects, including
construction of dozens of buildings and hundreds of miles of
roads. There was a dark side to the Roblin legacy, however,
and it involved a system of kick-backs and corruption which
resulted in the scandal that ended the political careers of
Coldwell, two cabinet colleagues, and the premier himself.

In 1913 the Roblin government entered into a contract for construction of a new legislative building. The cost of the project quickly grew because of what the government said were necessary changes made to the original design. Rumours of fraud became so prevalent that provincial Liberals demanded a Royal Commission to investigate the allegations. When Roblin refused those demands the province's lieutenant governor exercised his constitutional authority and on 25 April 1915 appointed one. Four months later the Commission issued its report. It found overwhelming evidence that Coldwell, Roblin, Minister of Public Works Walter Montague and Neepawa's James Howden, the province's former attorney general, had entered into a conspiracy to loot the provincial treasury, and that as of the date of the commission's report more than $800,000 already had been taken.

Three days after the report was made public warrants were issued for the arrest of the four politicians; and on August 31st they were arrested, formally charged with conspiracy to defraud, and then released on bail. After a month long preliminary inquiry all were committed to stand trial. Before it got underway the following July, however, Montague had died and Roblin and Howden were in failing health. From July 26th until the trial ended in early September the jury sat for six days a week and heard overwhelming evidence of the existence of a plot to create a campaign fund, by adding to the cost of work done on the project money which was then paid by the contractor to the Conservative party's chief organizer.

In his charge to the jury Mr. Justice Prendergast made clear that while there was much less evidence implicating Roblin than there was with regard to his former ministers, the conclusion reached by jurors about the fate of one of the accused must be the fate of the others. When jury members were interviewed after the trial ended they neither confirmed nor denied that this influenced their decision. What they did confirm, however, was that their vote was 9-3 in favour of conviction. Unconfirmed was that the vote to convict Coldwell was 11-1.

By the time a new trial was set to get underway on October 28th it had become apparent that Roblin and Howden were unlikely to survive another protracted proceeding. On 25 June 1917 charges against the alleged conspirators were dismissed. Before the year ended Howden did die, although Roblin regained his health and lived another twenty years.

George Robson Coldwell returned to Brandon and the practice of law. He died on 24 January 1924 and is buried in the Brandon cemetery. ✦

## CHAPTER 5

# the forgotten

IT IS A SAD REALITY THAT ONLY A FEW OF US ARE REMEMBERED after our death, despite the fame and attention we might have attracted while alive. Hugh Dyer was a general, war hero and friend of a king, but now lies in an over-grown plot in a rural graveyard. Paul Wolos did not live long enough to gain fame, but on an anonymous Viet Nam battlefield he made the ultimate sacrifice. Also sad are forgotten cemeteries. Nearly 2,000 Canadians lie abandoned in a farm field mere yards from a busy highway, with little to mark their passing. Equally lost to history are the men and women who died in Souris City, a community again part of the bush out of which it was carved in the waning years of the nineteenth century.

In memory of
BRIG. GEN. HUGH MARSHALL
DYER. C.B., C.M.G. D.S.O.
WHO DIED DEC. 25. 1938
AGED 78 YEARS
AND OF
F.O. JOHN PHILIP DYER D.F.C.
KILLED IN ACTION.
MAY 21. 1940
AGED 27 YEARS

# 1861-1938

# HUGH MARSHALL DYER

The war heroes many small-town Manitobans remember, if at all, usually come from away, from somewhere else. And so it is with one of the most decorated and brave soldiers to survive the carnage of World War I. Although his mother was a cousin of a British prime minister, his brother the friend of a prince and the man himself regarded with fondness by a king, he now lies largely forgotten in a cemetery in southwestern Manitoba.

Hugh Marshall Dyer was born on 28 January 1861 in Kingston, County Cork, Ireland, but lived most of his early life in the south of England. His father saw service with the British navy in the Baltic and fought in the Chinese opium war and against the slave trade on the west coast of Africa. Hugh's brother was also a naval captain and trained with the future King George V.

Soon after his birth Hugh's name was entered at The Royal Navy College in the expectation that he would follow in the footsteps of his father and brother. When it came time to write his entrance exam, however, he was sick with the measles and unable to attend. Forced to seek another occupation, he finished his education and taught school until 1881, when he emigrated to Manitoba.

The twenty-two-year-old Dyer immediately took up a homestead and started farming, sowing his first crop by hand. He filed on another quarter as a preemption, which increased his holding to 320 acres of scrub and bushland.

By the time he paid for and proved up his land the now married Dyer had grown concerned about the education his boys would receive if they stayed in the Franklin district, so in the winter of 1900 he sold out and bought a farm northeast of Minnedosa.

Dyer was a progressive farmer and active in community affairs. When Minnedosa's Lady Minto Hospital was established he sat on its first board. In addition to serving as a director and president of the local agricultural society, he was a member of the board of the Western Empire Life Association; and he and a brother-in-law managed elevators at Bethany, Minnedosa and Basswood. Dyer was also one of the founders of the Manitoba Agricultural College, and in the years preceding World War I he was chairman of its board.

But above all else Dyer was a soldier. In 1903 a unit of the Manitoba Dragoons was organized in Minnedosa, and he became an officer; when the 'Fighting Fifth' was organized at Valcartier eleven years later Major Dyer was appointed second in command.

Because the telephone wires connecting the trench with headquarters had been cut by German shell fire, Dyer and another soldier were tasked with carrying a message ordering the Battalion to fall back.

In his history of the Canadian Expeditionary Force, Sir Max Aitken, Lord Beaverbrook, said that he regarded one of Dyer's exploits to be among the most brave of any which occurred in World War I. During a particularly fierce confrontation the position of the 5th Canadian Battalion had become untenable. Because the telephone wires connecting the trench with headquarters had been cut by German shell fire, Dyer and another soldier were tasked with carrying a message ordering the Battalion to fall back.

Each received a copy of the order, since it was unlikely both would survive. Machine gun fire swept the ground around them as they scrambled in and out of the pot holes made by enemy shelling. One hundred yards from the trench Dyer's companion was shot through the side. Dyer went on, and was within feet of the trench when he was hit in the chest. He was able to deliver the message, however, and what was left of the Battalion fell back.

The wound Dyer suffered was sufficiently serious that in the hospital he was put aside in a cot and left to die. A doctor, and member of the British nobility, was walking through the ward when he noticed Dyer. Turning to those walking with him he nodded in the direction of the Canadian and said "He'll not live to get up out of that cot."

The dozing soldier heard the remark and raised himself on an elbow. "You're a liar, and be damned to you. I'll get up out of this cot here, and will see you die before me!"

Dyer did indeed recover. He was promoted to Brigadier-General and in July 1917 took command of the 7th Brigade. It consisted of the Princess Pats, the Royal Canadian Regiment, the 42nd Royal Highlanders of Canada and the 49th Edmonton Regiment. His reputation as a caring leader, already well-known, was enhanced when he immediately adopted the habit of writing the parents of every one of his men who had been killed or wounded in action. His compassion earned him the nickname Daddy.

By the time the war ended Dyer had been mentioned in dispatches five times. He was also awarded the Distinguished Service Order, a bar to the order, and made a Companion of the Most Distinguished Order of St. Michael & St. George and a Companion of the Most Honourable Order of the Bath.

When hostilities ceased in 1918 Dyer returned to his farm. In the waning days of December 1938 he contracted a serious cold and died two weeks later, on Christmas Day. The seventy-eight-year-old widower was preceded by a younger brother, who also died on Christmas Day.

Brigadier-General Dyer was buried with full military honours. Although Minnedosa's Legion Hall is named for him, and a stained glass window in St. Mark's Church is a permanent memorial to his memory, today few town residents know his story. He is buried in the Minnedosa cemetery. ◆

His reputation as a caring leader, already well-known, was enhanced when he immediately adopted the habit of writing the parents of every one of his men who had been killed or wounded in action.

# 1947-1967

## PAUL HARVEY WOLOS

PFC PAUL HARVEY
WOLOS USMC
BORN IN PORT ARTHUR ONT.
JULY 22, 1947
DIED ON FOREIGN SOIL
FOR FREEDOM
APRIL 28, 1967

NOW SAFE IN THE ARMS OF JESUS

During the Vietnam War more than 12,000 Canadians saw active service in the armed forces of the United States. Of that number one hundred and ten were killed. One of them was from Brandon.

Paul Harvey Wolos was born in Port Arthur, Ontario (now Thunder Bay) on 22 July 1947 but by the time he enlisted in the United States Marine Corps as a private first class he and his family were living on McDonald Avenue in Brandon's west end. Paul's tour of duty started on 31 March 1967 in Quang Tin Province and ended twenty-eight days later during Operation Union.

Operation Union was a search and destroy mission launched on 21 April 1967 in a densely populated and rice-rich valley considered essential to the ability of the North Vietnamese Army to control South Vietnam's five northern provinces. The Fifth Marine Regiment in which Wolos served was an experienced force that had fought in Vietnam since its arrival in the summer of 1966, and it was assigned to the valley to support the outnumbered South Vietnamese Army.

The action that resulted in the death of Wolos started when a reinforced marine company began a sweep towards a communist held village. When it came into contact with units of the North Vietnamese Army, and was pinned down in a tree line near its objective, elements of the 3rd Battalion were dispatched by helicopter to support them. While the main body of the reinforcements fought into a communist-held village to engage the NVA, other elements landed from helicopters east of the battlefield to block the enemy's most likely escape route. By the next morning the North Vietnamese had been driven out of the enemy village.

Wolos's unit was assigned the mission of pursuing the fleeing enemy and destroying its fighting forces and their supplies. When contact was finally made, fighting was so intense that it was four days before the first of the wounded could be evacuated. Prior to the start of the battle Wolos had been advised that, as a foreign-born member of the Marines, he could not be forced to engage in active combat. He refused to serve with a support unit, however, and on April 28th he became the only member of K Company to be killed during the confrontation.

Although he died almost forty years ago, Paul's memory lives on in the hearts and minds of both those with whom he served, and friends and family members. In June 2003 his company commander posted a message on a website established by the American military to honour those killed during the Vietnam War. "That night of 28 April we slept in an open field that was heavily boobie trapped. As we started taking casualties and evacuated two of our wounded you stepped on a bouncing betty and were mortally wounded. We tried to confort and make you feel better but the corpsman could

not do much for you. We put you in a helicopter that flew you back to the hospital in Chu Lai. We prayed that you would be saved but your death was my first combat casualty and I never forgot you. We the members of K/3/5 think of you every year when we have our reunions. We all remember you and wish you would have survived. You were a very fine Marine. Semper Fidelis."

The message prompted Paul's brother to post one of his own. "After 37 years the pain of losing my brother has not dulled. I have often wondered who was with Paul and whether or not Paul was alone at the time of his death. I now know he was with his Marine buddies and he was looked after to the best of everyone's ability. I know Paul had a very strong sense of loyalty to the Marine Corps and was very proud to be a Marine. Paul died for a cause he believed in, and for a country he had love and respect for."

Among the other messages posted on the website is one from Joan, a high school classmate of Paul's. It reads simply "Always remembered."

Paul Wolos is buried in Thunder Bay's St. Andrew's Cemetery beside his father and mother. ✦

# 1891-1960

## BRANDON ASYLUM FOR THE INSANE CEMETERY

Almost two thousand people are buried in one of Manitoba's largest abandoned cemeteries, their passing marked only by a cairn bearing the names of women and men now largely forgotten. All were patients of the Brandon Asylum for the Insane.

It opened in 1890 as a provincial reformatory for boys. Staffed by a governor, chief attendant and a matron, all supervised the building's lone occupant, a nine-year old boy serving a five year sentence for stealing undelivered mail. A year later the provincial government decided to make better use of the facility, and re-designated the reformatory as an asylum for the insane. In July 1891 the institution admitted its first patients, twenty-nine men and women transferred from the Provincial Gaol and the Selkirk Asylum.

Within months the mental health centre's first burial ground, located east and slightly south of its main building, was in use. Over the next twenty-five years nearly five hundred patients were interred, not a surprising number considering the state of health of those admitted. Many patients were already near death when they entered the facility and died within days of their admission. Others were mentally healthy but old and infirm. In one year alone their deaths represented nearly half of the centre's mortality rate, perhaps from what we now identify as Alzheimer's disease.

The most publicized death of a mental health centre patient ironically did not occur on hospital grounds.

Most men and women who died, however, were victims of contagious diseases which flourished because of over-crowding and the physical intimacy associated with well over a thousand people having to share common cooking, sleeping and bathroom facilities. In 1908, for instance, more people died from tuberculosis than from any other cause.

But the deaths of some had nothing to do with natural causes. Accidents, suicides and even acts of violence were not uncommon. The first 'unnatural' death occurred in 1896. After two patients were temporarily left on their own in the institution's cow barn some kind of dispute aroused the anger of one and he struck his companion on the head with an axe, killing him. At the inquest an asylum doctor testified that he was surprised at the actions of the murderer. Although the offender was known to be dangerous, said the doctor, he had always been "perfectly harmless when alone!"

The most publicized death of a mental health centre patient ironically did not occur on hospital grounds.

Shortly before supper on 4 November 1910 a fire started in the garret of the facility's central building, and within hours it had engulfed the entire structure. All 643 patients escaped the conflagration and were herded into a cattle corral before being bedded down in a variety of livestock barns. Although a detachment of special policemen were stationed along the approaches to the city to prevent inmates from escaping, a forty-eight-year-old female patient, described as educated and refined, walked undetected from the hospital to a small body of water on the grounds of the Experimental Farm. She survived the night, but her lifeless body was found the next day by a group of boys skating on the pond.

The last burial on the grounds of the Brandon Mental Health Centre took place in the 1960s. ✦

# 1880-1989

## SOURIS CITY

Between 1870 and 1880 towns and villages sprang up all over western Manitoba. Although most settlements consisted of small groups of families and friends, and survived only a few years, virtually all had a burial area. Once these settlers moved on, the homes they abandoned quickly crumbled to nothingness, and their cemeteries were slowly overgrown by the prairie from which they had been so painstakingly carved. Within a few years former inhabitants would have been hard-pressed to find the spot where a loved one lay at rest. And so it was with Souris City.

Located 40 kilometres southeast of Brandon, the community was established in 1880 by Toronto contractors William Scott and his son, William J. They gambled that a branch line would soon be run south from the Canadian Pacific Railway's main line, and they had a townsite surveyed on land they purchased along the Souris River. Settlers from Ontario, the Maritimes and even Great Britain were attracted by promises of free land and soil capable of producing yields of more than forty bushels per acre.

The first to arrive lived in tents until building materials could be brought by flat bottom barges to the junction of the Assiniboine and the Souris river, and then hauled by ox cart to the settlement. But supplies were scarce, and many settlers lived in homes made out of sod and whatever else could be either bought or scrounged. By 1882 Souris City consisted of a boarding house, black-smith shop, a school that also doubled as a church, a steam-powered grist mill, a brick manufactory, a hotel and two stores. Even the *Manitoba Free Press* noticed the progress being made by the small community, and it said that no one should doubt the town's future. Unsaid but equally true was that no one doubted the need for a cemetery, and within months of its establishment a drowning victim became the burial ground's first resident.

In the early 1880s the CPR's agreement with the federal government prevented anyone else from constructing a railway in much of western Manitoba. When the provincial Liberal party under Thomas Greenway took power in Manitoba in 1888 it announced that it was going to break the CPR's monopoly, and that the construction of a southern branch line would start immediately. In Souris City signs reading 'Railway Competition Has Come' welcomed Greenway and 2,000 other people to a picnic celebrating the end of the CPR's monopoly. The celebration, however, was premature.

When a branch line of the Northern Pacific and Manitoba Railway was built in 1889 it crossed the Souris River five kilometres downstream of Souris City. Overnight the community died. Most of the town's buildings were hauled to the newly created village of Wawanesa, and the rest were abandoned. Unlike Manitoba, some provinces have statutes which deal with cemeteries abandoned under such circumstances. The Cemeteries Protection Act of Nova Scotia, for instance, allows people to trespass on private property to preserve cemeteries which are no longer being managed and used for burials.

Such has not been the case in Souris City, however, where only a single concrete base, forgotten but hauntingly romantic, can be seen among overgrown weeds and thorns in an isolated bush on the farm of Sheila and Brad Cline. The opening stanza of Thomas Gray's "Elegy Written in a Country Churchyard," from 1768 captures a village's dead spirit:

The curfew tolls the knell of parting day,
The lowing herd wind slowly o'er the lea,
The ploughman homeward plods his weary way,
And leaves the world to darkness and to me. ✦

THE HICKMAN FAMILY SUFFERED THREE TRAGEDIES when the Titanic sank. Equally tragic was the death of the Wheat City's first police chief, a man killed by a gun no one fired. All train wrecks are likely preventable, but none seemed more so than the accident that took the lives of nineteen men when two trains collided at little more than walking speed. Like the men on the snow train, Lloyd Shields had no sense of his impending fate, even as the bomb that killed him fell onto an open-air dance floor. Far less perfect was the fire that destroyed the Olympia Café, taking the life of the only firefighter in Brandon's long history to die fighting a blaze. More than three decades earlier an even more disastrous fire struck western Manitoba when seven members of a threshing crew died in the loft of a hay barn. William Curle also died in a farm accident, but he was the victim not of a fire but of a bridge that collapsed under the weight of his own steam engine. Louis Slotin died in an industrial accident. In his case the industry involved the manufacture of atom bombs.

# CHAPTER 6
# accidents & disasters

IN LOVING MEMORY OF
LEWIS HICKMAN.
AGED 32 YRS.
BELOVED HUSBAND OF
MARIE HICKMAN.
ALSO OF
LEONARD MARK HICKMAN.
AGED 24 YRS. AND
STANLEY GEORGE
HICKMAN AGED 21 YRS.
SONS OF HERBERT & EMILY
HICKMAN FRITHAM HAUTS.
ENGLAND VICTIMS OF THE TITANIC
DISASTER APR. 15. 1912.
Until the day breaks and the shadows fly away

HICKMAN

# 1879-1912

## LEWIS HICKMAN

The 256th victim of the Titanic disaster pulled from the icy waters of the Atlantic in April 1912 was born in Hampshire, England. His younger brother had emigrated to the Neepawa area in 1908 and when he returned home for Christmas three years later he persuaded his two brothers to join him in Canada. The three men boarded the Titanic on 10 April 1912. When the giant ocean liner struck an iceberg two days later Lewis Hickman grabbed the coat of his brother Leonard and made his way to the deck. When his body was recovered it was identified as that of Leonard because Leonard's Forester's Lodge membership card was found in a pocket.

The Hickmans and their travelling companions had virtually no chance of survival after the liner began to fill with water. The Titanic's twenty lifeboats could carry only one third of the ship's passengers and crew, and because women and children took priority more than 90 per cent of male second-class passengers were doomed either to drown or to die of hypothermia.

When Leonard's lodge brothers in Neepawa learned that his body had been found they had it shipped from Halifax to Neepawa for burial. The body arrived an hour before the funeral was to begin, but when the casket was opened no one had any idea who the occupant was. Leonard was dark and clean shaven, while the well-preserved body lying in front of them was that of an older, fair-haired man who wore a moustache. Because the church was packed with people waiting for the funeral to begin it was decided to seal the casket and allow the service to proceed. Only after the personal effects thought to belong to Leonard were returned to England did the wife of Lewis learn that it was her husband and not Leonard who was interred in Canada.

Among the stories which grew out of the Titanic disaster was one associated with Percy Deacon, the youngest of four friends who travelled with the Hickmans. He was engaged to be married to a sister of the brothers, and borrowed his share of the fare from their father. Shortly after news of the sinking reached England, Mr. Hickman Sr. showed up at the home of Deacon's parents, demanding re-payment of the loan.

One thousand five hundred and twenty-three people drowned when the Titanic sank. Within days 328 bodies were recovered, including that of Lewis. Although most passenger ships avoided the site of the sinking in the weeks after the disaster, some could not and a number of instances were reported where bodies were struck by ships and knocked several feet into the air. Passengers on one liner reported seeing the body of a woman in her night dress, clasping a baby to her breast, floating beside the body of another woman whose arms surrounded a shaggy dog. A month after the sinking and 200 miles from the Titanic's last position the Oceanic came upon a collapsible lifeboat containing three bodies. For some unknown reason the canvas sides of the boat had never been raised.

The bodies of one hundred and sixteen Titanic victims were buried at sea, 59 were claimed by friends or relatives and shipped to other locations, and 150 were buried in three Halifax cemeteries. Of those recovered, 128 were unidentified. ✦

Only after the personal effects thought to belong to Leonard were returned to England did the wife of Lewis learn that it was her husband and not Leonard who was interred in Canada.

# 1957

# THE MANITOBA POWER COMMISSION EXPLOSION

September in Manitoba is arguably the most pleasant month of the year, as the long hot days of summer slowly give way to the cool, crisp days of fall. For the residents of Brandon, Friday 13th of September 1957 was that kind of day: calm with a bright sun, and no suggestion of the devastation that was about to claim the lives of two city men.

By 4:00 pm the workday of employees of the Manitoba Power Commission was rapidly winding down. Most office staff had finished their last coffee break of the day and were back at work, when five latecomers walked into the building's canteen. As Lewis Stouffer began pouring himself a cup of coffee, Kelvin Gerry moved to the front of the cupboard, leaving Irv Powers, Tom Tawes and Fred Morden to wait for their turn at the urn. Suddenly, and with no warning, the whole world changed.

A huge explosion blew out the bottom of the smokestack, rocking the building and bringing down tons of rubble. Stouffer was thrown to the floor and scalded with coffee from the overturned urn. Gerry, standing in front of the cupboard, was knocked off his feet and a cupboard door fell on his back, protecting him from serious injury. Powers was not so lucky. Although he too ended up on the floor, a heavy beam landed on his back, crushing his spine. Tawes, a thirty-two-year-old father of two, and Morden, a year younger and also the father of two, both died under tons of rubble.

The three survivors were immediately rushed to the Brandon General Hospital, where it was quickly determined that while Stouffer and Gerry could be treated locally, the much more seriously injured Powers required specialized surgery and should be taken to Winnipeg. Construction on both the Trans-Canada highway and Highway 2 made the trip by ambulance impossible, and Powers's doctors decided to keep him overnight before sending him to the province's capital by train.

The badly injured hydro worker arrived in Winnipeg the next morning, having been transported in a CPR baggage car accompanied by Jean Laco, a Brandon nurse. He was met by an ambulance crew who wanted to move him from his back board to a gurney before transporting him to the hospital. Ms. Laco, the nurse who accompanied Powers on the trip was concerned that the procedure might further damage his spine, and threatened to call another ambulance if her patient was not transported as he was. Powers has always credited the care given him by Ms. Laco during the trip to Winnipeg and her dealing with the ambulance crew, with preventing further damage to his spine.

In the end Powers spent six months in hospital, the first three in a sling, which allowed him to be turned every couple of hours. After his surgery Powers could walk, but the accident ended his promising future as a baseball player. His involvement with the Brandon Cloverleafs continued, however, this time in the capacity as coach and manager.

Within days of the explosion an inquest was held to determine the cause of the accident and the deaths of Tawes and Morden. After a careful examination of the site, and lengthy interviews with those who witnessed the tragedy, the inquest panel concluded that there had been no carelessness or dereliction of duty on anyone's part, and that the accident occurred when a pocket of gas had built up near the base of the smokestack and ignited.

Stouffer, Gerry and Powers all continued their careers at the Manitoba Power Commission. In recognition of his contribution to the sport of baseball, in 1997 Powers was inducted into Manitoba's Baseball Hall of Fame. He was also inducted into the Manitoba Softball Hall of Fame in 2004.

The funerals of the two men were held on September 16th, Tawes's from First Baptist Church and Morden's from St. Paul's United. Both were buried at Westlawn Memorial Gardens, now Rosewood Memorial Gardens. ✦

# 1846-1885

## ARCHIBALD
## L. MCMILLAN

In the late nineteenth century funerals were big events in towns like Brandon, and it was not usual for an entire community to turn out if the person being buried was particularly prominent. At least that was the case for the city's first chief of police. What was unusual, however, was that a month after he was buried in Manitoba his body was disinterred and transported to Guelph, Ontario, where he was buried a second time, after another large and open-casket service.

By the time Archibald McMillan accidentally shot himself in a Brandon hardware store, he had already spent the greater part of his life as a police officer. The thirty-nine-year-old started his career in law enforcement in Chatham, Ontario, rising through the ranks to the position of sergeant. From there he went to Guelph, where he was chief of the town's police force before quitting to become a local agent for the California book publisher, Lyon's & Co.

McMillan quickly grew bored with his new job, and in early spring 1882 re-entered law enforcement, this time in Winnipeg. A few months later he was hired as Brandon's chief constable, joining Donald Campbell and John Keays as the city's first police force.

In the 1880s Brandon was not an easy place to enforce the law. Not only was the police chief the community's fire and health inspector, he had to deal with the dozens of young farmers and railway labourers who regularly came to town for the dual pleasures of drink and companionship. Conflict was a constant, and McMillan had quickly proven that he could handle it "without fear, favour or affection."

The chief was an imposing figure. He was slightly over six feet tall with a compact, muscular build and a sharp eye and stern expression. Even more impressively, he was sober, intelligent and hard-working. But he was not careful.

December 16th, 1885 was a Wednesday. Just before noon McMillan entered the hardware store of the town's mayor to buy a loader for a rifle he had seized from a rowdy a few months earlier. To ensure that he got exactly what he wanted the chief brought the gun with him. He was putting it back into its cloth case when it became stuck. Without thinking, McMillan tapped the butt of the rifle on the floor as he bent over its muzzle to free it from its case.

The slight tap was enough to discharge the cartridge he had left in the chamber, and the bullet passed through his abdomen to lodge in the store's ceiling. McMillan seemed almost startled by the explosion, and for a moment stood motionless, looking at his stomach. Then without saying a word, he collapsed onto the floor.

> Without thinking, McMillan tapped the butt of the rifle on the floor as he bent over its muzzle to free it from its case.

Although Dr.'s Macdonald, McDiarmid and Fleming, the city's entire medical community, arrived on the scene within minutes, it was clear to everyone that the wound was mortal.

McMillan was helped to a nearby chair, where he waited in intense pain to say goodbye to his wife and son. During the time between the accident and their arrival he was asked if he needed to put his affairs in order. He said that he did not and that, although he had no will, "everything was in a satisfactory shape."

Moments after speaking with his wife and son, McMillan died. His body was immediately taken to his residence at the corner of 9th Street and Rosser Avenue, where members of the town's Masonic Lodge took charge of both his remains and his funeral arrangements.

Two days later local Masons and Oddfellows, together with members of the town's band, began assembling for the afternoon's proceedings. They were to lead a procession past a raised platform on Rosser Avenue, where the chief's body was to rest in an open casket. Ceremonies got underway at 3:00 pm and thirty minutes later the band, at the head of a procession over a mile long and playing the 'Dead March from Saul,' passed the coffin of the city's former police chief, "whose spirit, in its flight, had left behind a calm and natural look upon that well-known countenance."

For a month the remains of McMillan lay buried in the Brandon cemetery. Then in early January 1886 they were disinterred and shipped to Guelph. On its arrival the coffin of the former chief was placed in a corridor outside the town's police court, where locals could pay their respects. Early in the afternoon of Sunday, January 24th McMillan's body was taken to St. Andrews Church, where his coffin was draped in black and placed in front of the pulpit.

When the service ended the cover of the casket was removed so that those present, including the hundreds who stood outside listening to the ceremonies, could view the body of a man who had once lived among them. It took forty-five minutes for nearly one thousand people to file past the coffin. According to a Guelph newspaper, McMillan's features "had not changed much from the time of his first interment, and his old friends and acquaintances could easily recognize them."

It turned out that McMillan had reason to tell those who were present when he died that his affairs were in order. His wife was the sole beneficiary of a $12,000 life insurance policy, an enormous sum for the time. Unfortunately, she did not live long enough to enjoy it. The former Maggie Stewart died just over three years after her husband. The two are buried beside each other in Guelph's Woodlawn Memorial Park. ✦

According to a Guelph newspaper, McMillan's features "had not changed much from the time of his first interment, and his old friends and acquaintances could easily recognize them."

# 1916
## BRANDON TRAIN WRECK

MCGHIE

IN LOVING MEMORY OF
GEORGE McGHIE
DIED JANUARY 12, 1916
AGED 42 YEARS.
GODS FINGER TOUCHED HIM AND HE SLEPT.

**W**ednesday January 12, 1916, was a bitterly cold day in Brandon. Over night the temperature had dropped to forty-four below Fahrenheit, and the men hired by the Canadian Pacific Railway to clear snow dumped in its east-end rail yard on the weekend were making slow progress. Most were eastern Europeans, like Ignace Kircharski, whose wife had given birth to the couple's seventh child the evening the storm hit.

Three snow trains were working in the yard, each with a fifty-man crew. Just before 10:00 am the unit Kircharski was helping load finished its first run and backed onto the main line for another pick-up. Snow trains typically have no schedule and operate under the control of a section foreman or yardmaster.

Because company rules forbade work engines from using a passenger track when scheduled trains were in the area, Edward Beale, the conductor of the snow train, walked to the depot to make sure that nothing was due in from the west. Although assured that the schedule was empty, out of an abundance of caution he sent his brakeman to the train's caboose to watch for on-coming cars.

While George McGhie, foreman of the snow-clearing gang, told Beale where to pick up his next load, thirty day-labourers climbed

into the caboose to escape the cold. At the same moment an eight-car load of hogs from Calgary was finally cleared to depart for Winnipeg, six hours late. It had been delayed by a stalled freight, forcing it off its regular track onto the main passenger line. As the stock train inched forward its engineer was blinded by a dense cloud of smoke, steam and fog produced by a combination of other units working in the area, the yard's roundhouse and the nearby Assiniboine River.

Because yardmaster John Richardson had warned the engineer of the freight train about the presence of the snow crews, the east bound transport was travelling at less than eight kilometres an hour as it inched towards the city's Eighth Street bridge. The snow train, travelling in the opposite direction but on the same track, was pushing ten flatcars west, its caboose in the lead. Like the stock train, it was barely moving. Under normal conditions both could be stopped in a matter of feet, but conditions this day were anything but normal. Bad visibility was made worse by the fact that both trains were working their way through a tunnel of darkness caused by the stationery units on their either side, which blocked out the morning sun.

James Fairburn, the engineer of the freight, was the first to realize that it was on the same track as the snow train. As soon as he saw the caboose emerge out of the gloom a dozen

yards ahead he threw on his emergency brake, bringing his engine to a standstill. The brakeman in the cupola of the caboose reacted more slowly.

The impact went virtually unnoticed by those riding in the rear of the trains, but was strong enough to force the caboose back onto the attached flat-bed, bending it upward. The car immediately broke free of the track and telescoped forward, slicing through the caboose like a knife. Fourteen men were killed instantly and another five died in hospital. The collision was so severe that some of the dead were actually embedded into the wooden walls of the lead unit.

Rescuers lay the dead and dying along the track on blankets and mattresses as ambulances and hearses rushed to the scene. In a tragic twist of fate, it was later learned

The twelve-person jury held that the accident was caused by the negligence of the Canadian Pacific Railway, which had no procedure in place to ensure that trains did not travel through a railyard on the same track in opposite directions, and the inclement weather.

that some of the victims had actually survived the accident, but had frozen to death waiting to be rescued. Among the saddest of the morning's heart-wrenching scenes was the frantic effort of the seventeen-year-old son of Kircharski who, with frozen hands and feet, dug through the wreckage in a vain effort to save his father.

Before the day ended other tragedies were played out in each of the city's three funeral homes. Nothing could assuage the anguish of grief-stricken wives and mothers, who suddenly were left with only the cherished memory of loved ones lost.

The day after the accident a coroner's inquest was convened to determine who was at fault. In the end it held that both trains had been cleared to proceed, and that each crew had carried out its responsibilities exactly as it should have. The same, however, could not be said for their employer. The twelve-person jury held that the accident was caused by the negligence of the Canadian Pacific Railway, which had no procedure in place to ensure that trains did not travel through a railyard on the same track in opposite directions, and the inclement weather.

George McGhie was among the dead. The forty-year-old father of two was the only non-eastern European to die in Canada's ninth most devastating train wreck. He is buried in the Brandon cemetery. ✦

LLOYD SHIELDS
APRIL 23 1921
JULY 16 1943.
A loving son and brother
and a faithful friend

# 1921-1943

## LLOYD WESLEY SHIELDS

**D**uring the Second World War, summer evenings on the prairies were often a time to relax with friends, and an outdoor dance was a particularly welcome diversion from worries about friends and relatives fighting in Europe. On 16 July 1943, Irene Fletcher, the wife of an air force trainee, took advantage of the moment and organized a Red Cross fund-raising dance on her father's farm located south-west of Brandon. Neighbours arrived to the sight of a beautiful moon, the plaintive wail of a violin and the laughter of friends. No one could have imagined the tragedy that was about to take the life of one of their own.

Just before midnight everyone was to form up for a square dance. Hugh Ferguson, a member of the band, had just turned to speak to the pianist when chaos broke out. With a deafening roar and a blinding flash of light the corner of the dance floor exploded. As panic swept over the crowd Ferguson turned and saw Lloyd Shields lying over a gaping hole in the floor, a pool of blood spreading from

According to Isabel Ferguson, Irene Fletcher's sister, when the panic that followed the explosion finally lifted, revelers quickly noticed that dozens of people had been injured by flying shrapnel.

what seconds before had been his foot. Dropping his violin and kneeling beside his mortally wounded friend, Ferguson heard a weak "Take my shoes off Hugh." As Ferguson reached down he saw that his friend's left foot had been completely blown away in the explosion.

Above the panic stricken crowd a low flying plane began a slow turn. Fearing it was about to make a second run over the dance floor Ferguson shouted "Put out the lights" and, except for a single lamp held over Shields, everything went dark. To those milling about it was obvious that Shields was dying. As the closest friend of the victim, Ferguson was asked to fetch Shields parents, who lived on a neighbouring farm. While he was gone, others wounded in the attack were attended to. According to Isabel Ferguson, Irene Fletcher's sister, when the panic that followed the explosion finally

lifted, revelers quickly noticed that dozens of people had been injured by flying shrapnel. Since there was no ambulance service available the injured helped each other into cars for the trip to the Brandon hospital. For Ferguson the journey back to the Stanley farm was heartbreaking, made all the worse by the fact that Shields had already died when his parents finally arrived.

At the inquest that followed it was determined that the bomb which killed Shields was a ten-pound practice explosive dropped inadvertently by an RCAF trainer on its way to a bombing range four miles west of the scene of the accident. Lloyd Wesley Shields was twenty-three when he became the only Manitoban killed by a bomb dropped in Canada during the Second World War. He is buried in the Brandon cemetery. ✦

# 1953
## OLYMPIA CAFÉ FIRE

Although the first Monday in April 1953 started like any spring day in Brandon, by its end one of the city's largest blazes had taken the life of a fire fighter. Fred Brown was fifty-eight, a father of six and a twenty-four-year veteran when he became the first member of the Brandon Fire Department to die fighting a fire.

It was just after 1:00 pm when the first alarm rang. The Olympia Café, built at the corner of 10th Street and Rosser Avenue in 1883, had its dining room portion erected thirty-four years later. When the firefighters arrived they saw smoke pouring from the basement of this part of the building and fire rapidly spreading throughout the first and second floors.

Their equipment was too antiquated to deal with such dense smoke, with masks that were relics from World War II and did little to protect a wearer's lungs and eyes. Locating the source of the fire was further complicated by a basement maze of small storage rooms used by the building's various tenants.

The first firefighters were immediately forced back by heavy smoke. With additional masks they entered the basement for a second time, but were again forced back. Brown was with both groups, and his decision in the heat of the moment had fatal consequences.

The high regard with which firefighters generally, and Fred Brown specifically, were held was made evident at Brown's funeral.

In the 1950s fire department protocol dictated that, when entering a burning building, every fireman was to attach a life line to his belt to facilitate rescue in the event of an emergency. Brown ignored the protocol. When his colleagues regrouped after their second unsuccessful attempt to enter the basement they immediately noticed that Brown was not with them. By this time, however, the blinding smoke and intense heat made rescue impossible. Five hours elapsed before his body was recovered.

The high regard with which firefighters generally, and Fred Brown specifically, were held was made evident at Brown's funeral. Attendees included members of the Brandon City Police Department, the Brandon detachment of the RCMP, representatives from five Winnipeg fire departments, politicians from virtually every level of government, and members of the city's fire department. Civic offices in Brandon closed as Brown's flag-draped casket stood in a sea of floral tributes, many from fire departments throughout the province. When the funeral service ended a fire truck, on which a cross had been erected, carried the casket to Rosewood Memorial Gardens, where an honour guard lined both sides of the path leading to Brown's grave.

Frederick Brown is still the only fire fighter in the Brandon Fire Department to lose his life fighting a fire. ✦

# 1915

# ALEXANDER HARVEST FIRE

In September 1915 seven men lost their lives in what is thought to be the largest farm tragedy in Manitoba history. The fire took the lives of an entire Alexander threshing crew and burned so intensely that all that remained of the men were a handful of bones.

Following a late supper the men had retired for the night to the loft of a barn located less than a hundred yards from the home of Alfred Magee, who later testified that he had instructed them to sleep in a nearby granary which had been cleaned out for their use. His concern about the risk of fire in the loft was well founded, and within an hour all seven were dead.

Magee and members of his family were all sleeping when the glare from the burning barn woke them. The entire household, including a hired man and his wife, immediately rushed outside, shouting to the men in the loft. There was no response. When the spectators realized that there was nothing that could be done to help the harvesters they turned their attention to the livestock. Before a cow shed, piggery and hen house were destroyed they managed to save most of Magee's animals.

When Winnipeg's Radford & Wright door and sash factory was destroyed by a fire started by James Dodds, two fire fighters and five spectators died in an explosion which blew the building apart.

At the inquest held to examine the cause of the fire jurors were taken to the scene of the tragedy where two tables had been erected. On them were what remained of the seven men. Although the skulls of the victims were whole when the inquest began, as soon as an attempt was made to move them each, without exception, crumbled. All that remained were a few charred ribs and a single collar bone.

After hearing testimony from ten witnesses it took the district coroner and an inquest jury just twenty minutes to conclude that the deaths were the result of a tragic accident, and that the deceased must have been overcome by smoke since none had made any attempt to escape the fire. Although no blame was attached to anyone, the jurors noted "that the practice of men sleeping in barns is exceedingly dangerous and should be stopped by law."

In a strange twist of fate, Brandon and area had a connection with another fire that two years later also took the lives of seven people. When Winnipeg's Radford & Wright door and sash factory was destroyed by a fire started by James Dodds, two fire fighters and five spectators died in an explosion which blew the building apart. That fire was followed by others started by Dodds, including Emanuel Baptiste Church, a commercial warehouse and the Mason-Risch Piano building.

Dodds was eventually convicted of setting ten fires and sentenced to fifteen years in jail. Before he began serving his sentence, however, authorities concluded that he was mentally incompetent, and his arson convictions were stayed. Instead of Stony Mountain Penitentiary Dobbs was sent to Brandon, where he spent six years at the city's mental health facility. On his release he was immediately deported to Scotland. ✦

# 1842-1903

# WILLIAM CURLE

T hursday the 4th of September 1903 was an exciting day for William Curle. The prominent sixty-one-year-old farmer from the Aikenhead district (now Justice) had purchased a new Port Huron steam engine, the first steam tractor north of Brandon, to power his grain separator, and it was to be delivered that day.

Curle and his two sons had been eagerly awaiting delivery of the bulky machine. It was to replace an older, portable steam engine used to thresh grain, an operation which would begin as soon as the tractor was delivered. It actually had arrived in Brandon a day earlier. After being unloaded from a railroad flat car it was carefully checked over by Richard Chambers, a friend of William's and the agent for Port Huron.

Since everything was in order it was decided that Chambers would deliver the tractor to the Curle's farm the next day, and that he would be joined on the trip by the Curles, who were to drive to Brandon on wagons which were to haul the water and wood needed to provide the steam to drive the huge engine.

Six days after the accident the *Brandon Sun* suggested that the First Street Bridge had not been considered safe for heavy engines.

As the tractor steamed slowly along Rosser Avenue towards the First Street Bridge, Chambers asked his friend to join him on the steam engine. As Curle jumped down from the wagon he was urged by one of his sons not to get on the machine, at least until after it crossed the bridge. The son was concerned about the safety of the structure; but although William hesitated briefly, he shrugged off the admonition and climbed up with Chambers.

The steam engine climbed the approach and onto the bridge without incident, but as its rear wheels inched forward and the bridge began bearing the full weight of the tractor, there was a tremendous crash. Without warning the engine fell through the structure, turning upside down and landing on the two men, killing them instantly.

John Smith of Smithville had driven across the bridge as the tractor approached, and he glanced back just in time to see the tractor and its operators disappear. He immediately hurried to the police station, returning with the city's chief constable, who took charge of the rescue effort. Tackle was obtained and the tractor was raised enough to recover the badly crushed bodies of the two friends.

Six days after the accident the *Brandon Sun* suggested that the First Street Bridge had not been considered safe for heavy engines. Although the custom for operators of tractors like the one driven by Chambers and Curle was to carry heavy planks, which they placed lengthways on the bridge so that the engine could cross in safety, the newspaper noted that it was never intended that the bridge be used by heavy farm equipment.

Walter Shillinglaw was one of a number of witnesses who testified at the coroner's inquiry held a few days after the tragedy. The city engineer said that, although he had discovered that one of the bridge's supports was weaker than the others, he believed that the accident occurred because the tractor was driven too close to the edge of the bridge. He suggested that, had it crossed in the centre the machine and its operators would have gone over in safety. The coroner's jury agreed. It concluded that the accident was due solely to the weakness of one of the bridge joists, and that no one was at fault.

There is no evidence that warning signs had ever been installed on the bridge, suggesting to some Brandonites that the bridge had not been inspected on a regular basis. Two weeks after the death of Curle and Chambers, however, Brandon's municipal council passed a motion to have notices posted on both the city's First Street and Eighteenth Street bridges, advising that their use by steam engines was regulated by by-law.

The Port Huron tractor was raised from the bank below the bridge and quickly repaired. In an ironic twist, it was delivered to the Curle farm on the day of William's funeral, where it remained in use for the next thirty years.

William Curle was survived by his wife, four sons and three daughters. He is buried in the Humesville cemetery near Justice. Richard Chambers was also survived by his wife, and he is buried in the Brandon cemetery. ✦

TWO MEN IN WH
LEFT: W.J. JU
SUPERINTENDEN

# 1910-1946

# LOUIS ALEXANDER SLOTIN

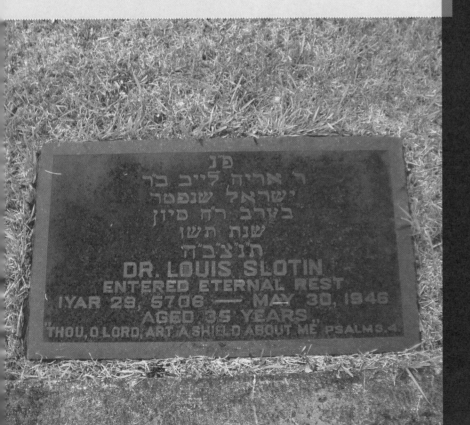

פנ
ר אריה לייב בר
ישראל שנפטר
בערב רח סיון
שנת תש
תנ"צב"ה
**DR. LOUIS SLOTIN**
ENTERED ETERNAL REST
IYAR 29, 5706 — MAY 30, 1946
AGED 35 YEARS
"THOU, O LORD, ART A SHIELD ABOUT ME" PSALM 3.4

When the world's first atomic bomb dropped on the Japanese city of Hiroshima on August 6th, 1945, it produced a flash of heat almost 1,000 times hotter than the sun, instantly vapourizing over 70,000 people. Three days later a second bomb devastated Nagasaki, forcing the surrender of Japan and bringing an end to World War II. The man responsible for determining the point at which the two weapons detonated was a young Winnipeg scientist who was to die at the hands of the very weapon he helped to create.

Louis Alexander Slotin was one of three children born to parents who came to Canada at the turn of the 20th century to escape the Czarist pogroms of White Russia. Slotin was academically gifted, entering the University of Manitoba when he was only sixteen. He was the first student in the school's history to graduate with a perfect mark in both chemistry and physics, and in 1934 earned a master's degree in the same disciplines. Two years later his doctoral thesis in bio-chemistry earned him an academic award for excellence from London University, and a six month job testing batteries for the Great Southern Railways in Dublin, Ireland.

In the years immediately preceding World War II Canadian governments had an unofficial policy of anti-Semitism, and when Slotin applied for a job with the country's National Research Council his application was rejected. Turning south, he accepted a position with the University of Chicago working on construction of one of the country's first cyclotrons. Building the atom-smasher was both hard and frustrating work. A lack of funding meant that Slotin and his colleagues not only did their own wiring and machining, they were even forced to help renovate the building in which the project was housed.

Slotin flourished in this chaotic environment. Papers he published in the field of radiobiology, together with his work on oscillitator circuits, brought him to the attention of the scientists in charge of constructing the world's first atomic bomb. Slotin joined the Manhattan Project's metallurgical laboratory in Chicago before moving to Tennessee and ultimately to Los Alamos, New Mexico.

By the end of 1944 Slotin had been placed in charge of criticality testing, a procedure which involved bringing fissile materials to near critical levels in order to establish their critical mass values. Slotin's experiments were known as 'tickling the dragon's tail.' He was such an accomplished practitioner at it that in the summer of 1945 he was tasked to assemble the core of Trinity, a precursor to the world's first nuclear weapon.

A year after World War II ended Slotin decided to leave the project, and on May 21st was demonstrating his technique of 'ticking the dragon's tail' to the scientist who was to replace him. Six other colleagues were in the lab, observing. Calculating critical mass required Slotin to screw two spheres of beryllium around a mass of fissionable material. The materials were lifeless if kept apart, but when brought together they would go critical, and a chain reaction would result.

Nine months earlier that is precisely what had happened when Slotin's laboratory assistant accidently dropped a tungsten carbide brick onto a plutonium core, creating a supercritical mass. Although he immediately removed the brick, that scientist was fatally irradiated and twenty-eight days later became the first person to die as a result of a nuclear accident.

In calculating critical mass a sophisticated piece of machinery was normally used in the procedure. Two small spacers placed between the two spheres prevented them from coming together and starting a nuclear reaction. Slotin, however, did not trust the machine and carried out the experiment by hooking his thumb in a small hole in the top of the upper sphere and lowering it onto the bottom shell.

To increase the neutron multiplication of the experiment Slotin also removed the two one-inch spacers, keeping the spheres apart with the blade of a screwdriver. Although he had carried out the procedure dozens of times before, this time things went terribly wrong. As Slotin brought the two half-globes together his screwdriver slipped, and the upper half fell into position around the lower mass of fissionable material.

The experiment immediately went critical. There was, however, neither an explosion nor any kind of sound. The only indication to those present that something was amiss was a faint bluish glow, the result of either ionization of the air or an optical illusion caused by a stimulation of nerves in the eyes.

Whether intentionally or instinctively, Slotin jerked his hand upward, separating the two hemispheres and stopping the reaction. In doing so he received a lethal dose of radiation. Ironically, Slotin was not only using the same materials that killed his friend and assistant, he was to die in the same room in the hospital.

Slotin lived for nine days, but he knew as soon as the accident happened that he was doomed. He sent his mother and father a telegram, advising them of what had happened.

When his condition started to deteriorate he had a nurse phone his parents and suggested that, since he could not visit Winnipeg, perhaps they would come to him.

While a U.S. Army DC-3 made its way north to pick up Israel and Sonia the body of their son continued to decompose from its massive dose of radiation. Huge blisters erupted on his hands and forearms, his intestinal tract became paralyzed, and one by one his bodily functions shut down. The minerals of his teeth eventually became so radioactive that they burned the soft tissues of his mouth and tongue.

Out of respect for Israel and Sonia Slotin's orthodox beliefs the American government arranged for the aircraft carrying the two of them, and the body of their son, to arrive in Winnipeg before sundown on the beginning of the Jewish Sabbath. Two days later nearly three thousand people came together on the front lawn of the Slotin's north end residence to celebrate the life of one of Winnipeg's most gifted heroes, later walking as a group to Rosh Pina Synagogue for his funeral.

Although Louis Slotin died on May 30th, 1946, his memory lives on. The 1989 movie *Fat Man and Little Boy,* starring Paul Newman and John Cusack, contained a scene describing his accident, and his story was described in a 1955 novel, a 1999 television documentary, and a sonata written in 2001. In addition, both a park in north Winnipeg and an asteroid have been named in his honour.

Louis Slotin is buried beside his parents in Winnipeg's Shaarey Zedek Synagogue Cemetery. He was thirty-six-years-old when he died. ✦

TO A GREATER OF LESSER DEGREE ALL DEATHS ARE TRAGIC, but never more so than when they come at the hands of someone else. Each of the men whose crimes are described in this chapter was hanged. Harry Green had been in Canada only a year when without provocation he suddenly shot his best friend. For John Krafchencko murder was less sudden than an inevitable conclusion to a life of crime. James McGrath's murder was, he said, the result of loving his wife too much. William Webb was also a wife-killer, but love was not an issue when he became the first person hanged in a Brandon gaol. Lawrence Gowland never married, but like McGrath and Webb his victim was both defenseless and a woman. Earle Nelson never murdered a single woman — he killed twenty-seven. The last victim mentioned in this chapter is an elderly farm wife whose violent death resulted in the only triple hanging in Manitoba history.

# CHAPTER 7

# the executed

# 1887-1915

## HARRY GREEN

**H**arry Green had been a hired hand in the Hartney district for exactly one month when he murdered his best friend with a shotgun blast to the head. He had been in Canada less than a year when, on 25 February 1915, he became the third person hanged in the Brandon jail.

When Green and twenty-four traveling companions left north London for Canada the stocky Englishman was twenty-eight. The group had been recruited by one of the several organizations looking for a cheap source of labour for prairie farmers. In hindsight it was clear that Green's first days in Winnipeg were a harbinger of what was to come. He refused to sign the mandatory contract under which he was expected to work, and his trip to the Baker farm near Hartney came only after a Winnipeg police magistrate ordered that he be arrested if he did not carry out the terms of his agreement.

Green started working for the Bakers in mid-April 1914. A week later Thomas Hill was also hired. Hill was about 50 years old and grew up in the district, which probably explained why his salary of $35 a month was $11 more than Green was paid. Despite differences in their ages and incomes, the two immediately became friends. That friendship, however, was about to come to an abrupt end.

Apart from the fact that he was wearing Hill's vest and carrying the dead man's watch, Green had appropriated virtually all of his friend's belongings.

May 17th was a Sunday, and the Bakers left for church around 10:30 am Thirty minutes later a neighbour heard two shotgun blasts. When the Bakers returned shortly after noon Green told them that Hill had left to take a better paying job near Reston. Nothing was heard of Hill for the next three days, and his friends decided to investigate his disappearance. As they walked around the Baker farm one of them noticed an abandoned well about 100 yards from the farm buildings. When he first peered into the darkness all he could see was a bundle of wire and part of a plough. He thought it odd, however, that so many bubbles were rising to the surface, and decided to take a closer look. Sixteen feet down, barely protruding from the water, was what looked like the heel of a man's shoe.

Green was arrested as soon as the body was identified. Apart from the fact that he was wearing Hill's vest and carrying the dead man's watch, Green had appropriated virtually all of his friend's belongings. He protested his innocence, however, and maintained that claim throughout the trial, which got underway six months later. For a week Brandon's largest courtroom was packed almost to suffocation with people anxious to watch the proceedings. Noticeably absent was Frank Hill, the brother of the murdered man, who sat in a nearby hallway throughout the hearing, weeping.

After five days of testimony the jury retired to consider its verdict. A little over an hour later they returned. As the jurors took their seats Green stared at each in turn, expressionless. When the foreman stood to announce the verdict his voice was barely audible, and like everyone else in the courtroom, Green leaned forward to hear what was being said. Only when Mr. Justice Galt ordered him to stand did the face of the now convicted murderer colour. After telling the jurors that he was in complete agreement with their decision, Galt turned to Green. Without preamble the judge noted that there was only one sentence for him to pass.

Between the end of his trial and the date of his execution Green appeared to take to heart Galt's suggestion that he use his time to make peace with God. Within weeks he confessed to murdering Hill on what he described was a

• Justice Galt

sudden impulse. There had been, he said, no ill feeling between the two men, and he knew his friend to be a good living and quiet man. "The only explanation I can give for my act is that, having led a bad life, I was possessed of a devil at the time."

It was once the tradition in Canada for the sheriff of the judicial district in which a condemned prisoner was held to perform the actual hanging. Over time, however, sheriffs began employing others to carry out executions, and between 1890 and 1912 that person had been John Radclive. When Radclive died the Canadian government offered the job to Arthur English, who was then an executioner serving in the Middle East. Members of the English family had been executioners in England for 300 years, and Arthur's uncle was in 1915 the country's official hangman.

On the morning of his execution Green walked unaided from his cell to the scaffold, and when he reached its top he immediately stepped onto the platform's trap door. He looked straight ahead as English first stooped to tie his ankles, then pulled a black hood over his head, and finally adjusted the noose. Less than ten seconds later the trap was sprung. While it is not known whether Green's body was left hanging for one hour, as was done in England, it is known that it was taken by the Salvation Army.

Harry Green is buried in an unmarked grave in the Brandon cemetery. Thomas Hill is interred in Hartney. ✦

# 1881-1914

## JACK KRAFCHENKO

The life and death of Jack Krafchenko had equal parts violent, farcical and macabre. That his actions resulted in the death of a former Brandon banker and the imprisonment of his lawyer also made them tragic. By the time Krafchenko entered the Bank of Montreal in the small community of Plum Coulee just after noon on 3 December 1913 he had already earned a well-deserved reputation as a violent thug. His bungled robbery and murder of the bank's manager suggested he had learned nothing from a life of crime.

Although born in Romania of Ukrainian parents, Krafchenko grew up in Plum Coulee. For seventeen years his father worked as the town's blacksmith, and to most residents the idea that someone local would rob a bank in a town with a population of 150 people made no sense. What made it preposterous, however, was the fact that three weeks before the second robbery Krafchenko told a Bank of Montreal clerk, with whom he happened to be drinking, of his plans. He then committed the crime wearing a disguise so obviously false that he was recognized before he even walked into the bank, and during his escape he on three separate occasions left behind a bag of the money he had just stolen.

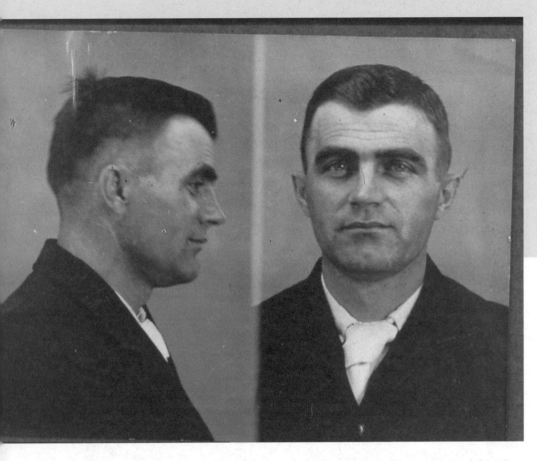

• Jack Krafchenko

admonition apparently had little effect, and four years later he was jailed for stealing a bicycle.

In 1902 the hard-drinking Krafchenko began touring rural Manitoba and Saskatchewan as a speaker on the evils of alcohol, passing enough bad cheques along the way to earn a sentence of eighteen months in Prince Albert Penitentiary. Within weeks, however, he escaped from a work detail and began robbing banks in Manitoba, the United States and Europe. In 1906 he returned to his home town and promptly robbed its branch of the Bank of Hamilton. He was eventually arrested and sentenced to three years in Stony Mountain Penitentiary.

Following his release Krafchenko briefly lived in northern Ontario before returning to Manitoba. Although he resided in Winnipeg, the boy from Plum Coulee spent a considerable amount of time in the town in which he grew up. In November he began talking to friends and drinking companions of his intention to rob the Bank of Montreal. A month later, apparently to the surprise of no one, he did.

Krafchenko made his escape in a car he had hired to wait for him a block from the bank. Two commercial travelers were standing outside the vehicle talking to its driver when Krafchenko showed up carrying several bags of money and wearing an obviously false beard. In fact it was precisely because his disguise was so ridiculous, and because he did

Krafchenko was eleven when he committed his first crime. His defence, that he thought the five watches he had taken were about to fall off their rack and that he was only keeping them until he had a chance to return them to the store's owner, might have worked. He was released from custody with a stern warning to refrain from stealing. The

One hundred and twenty miles west his victim, Henry Medley Arnold, had already been interred in the Brandon cemetery after one of the largest funerals in the city's history.

not stop to pick up the bag of money he dropped getting into the car, that the men were not alarmed. As both were to testify, they thought that the robber was a fake Santa Claus on his way to deliver flyers.

Krafchenko had his driver stop on one of the roads leading out of Plum Coulee. He then got out of the car, leaving a bag of money under the car's rear seat. After making his way to Winnipeg he spent much of the next week in his favourite Main Street bars. On December 9th, after asking one of his drinking companions to hide some of his stolen money, Krafchenko returned to the room he had rented in the name of a college professor. The following morning he was arrested.

After spending a month in jail, with the help of his lawyer, a jail guard and two other accomplices, he escaped from custody. The escape had actually been set for a day earlier, but Krafchenko's lawyer had gotten drunk in a bar and forgot to pick him up. The fugitive was re-captured on January 18th and his murder trial got underway in Morden two months later. On Thursday, 9 July 1914, a few seconds before 7:00 am, he was hanged in Winnipeg's Vaughan Street jail.

In a macabre postscript Krafchenko's stepmother claimed his body immediately after he was officially declared dead. She and five helpers then tried to bring her dead son back to life. Among those in attendance were two witches, a warlock, a soothsayer and a voodoo priest. Their efforts, however, were in vain, and Krafchenko was eventually buried in an unmarked Winnipeg grave. One hundred and twenty miles west his victim, Henry Medley Arnold, had already been interred in the Brandon cemetery after one of the largest funerals in the city's history. ✦

# 1908-1932

## JAMES MCGRATH

James McGrath was twenty-three when he murdered his wife in front of her mother and sister. After a brief marriage that produced one child and dozens of incidents of abuse he finally snapped. In a confession introduced at his trial he said that he killed her because he loved her. To prove it he hit her over the head with a shovel and stabbed her twenty-eight times.

Freda May Bloomfield was a teenager when she met this man and had just celebrated her twentieth birthday when she died. In the days leading up to her death she became determined to break out of the cycle of violence in which she found herself. On May 11th she finally left a note for her husband, telling him that she was going for good. James did not take the news well.

According to a witness who saw him later McGrath was running down a railway track, sobbing incoherently. He eventually made his way to the home of his mother-in-law, where he broke down completely. After crying for hours he lost any semblance of self-control and rolled off his chair onto the floor, helpless and hopeless.

McGrath responded by dropping the baby on the floor and rushing at the horrified woman, striking her over the head with the small shovel he had been concealing.

So complete was his collapse that his in-laws eventually called the local doctor. Ironically, he was the same man who three weeks later performed an autopsy on Freda. The doctor arrived to find McGrath in what he was to testify was a state of "extreme mental anguish." Although initially inclined to commit McGrath to Brandon's mental hospital, as the evening wore on the doctor was able to calm the distraught husband, and eventually felt comfortable that any danger he posed to himself or others had passed.

Over the next three weeks McGrath regularly walked in from his farm residence to see his wife and their infant son. Even after moving to Winnipeg he routinely made the journey, stealing rides on freight cars.

On June 2nd, however, something went awry. McGrath arrived at the home of his mother-in-law around 3:00 pm, but because it was raining his wife refused to let him take their son outside. McGrath came back when the rain stopped, and this time the infant was ready. When the two returned, McGrath said that he wanted to spend a little more time with his son, since he was on his way to Winnipeg.

Shortly after 6:00 pm he returned again, holding the baby in one hand and something behind his back with the other. He announced that he would no longer be visiting his son, since he was going away. He then asked his wife if she would change her mind and come back to him. Her answer sealed her fate.

She said no, there was no chance. McGrath responded by dropping the baby on the floor and rushing at the horrified woman, striking her over the head with the small shovel he had been concealing. Freda's sister was visiting in their mother's home and heard the racket. She hurried into the kitchen and attempted to grab her brother-in-law. In the ensuing struggle both sisters ended up on the floor, screaming for help.

Their mother heard their shouts and ran to see what was happening. She arrived just as Freda broke free and pushed her way out of the house through the kitchen door. When Mrs. Bloomfield attempted to prevent her son-in-law from going after her he hit her in the face, knocking out her front teeth.

McGrath caught up with his wife outside. He knocked her down and began striking her with two butcher knives he had grabbed off the kitchen counter. As blow after blow struck home the panicked woman pleaded with her husband, repeating over and over again "I will live with you, I will live with you."

While this was going on Freda's mother and sister ran to a nearby railway office. They told the yardmaster about the attack, and he immediately rushed to the Bloomfield residence. There he saw McGrath standing over his wife, stabbing her. As soon as the railroader yelled McGrath ran off.

He eventually arrived at the home of a married couple he knew. The woman noticed that he was covered in blood and asked him what had happened. When the out-of-breath McGrath gasped that he had just killed his wife, the husband told him to "beat it."

Within hours McGrath was arrested and confessed to the murder. He did not attend the inquest that followed, since he was overcome with emotion and teetering on the brink of a complete emotional breakdown. Five months later he was still an emotional wreck, but when his trial got underway in Brandon his attendance was not optional.

The trial lasted two days. McGrath did not testify, and no one was called on his behalf. The jury returned its verdict in just over two hours. After being in a state of near hysteria throughout the proceeding McGrath became calm and appeared almost relieved when he was sentenced to be hanged. Asked if he had anything to say, he replied that it was his hope "that my body shall be laid beside that of my wife as close as it can be."

McGrath murdered his wife on June 2nd, 1931 in Souris, Manitoba. He went to trial on November 17th, and just after 8:00 am on the first day of February 1932 he walked unassisted to the gallows. He was pronounced dead ten minutes after the trap sprung.

McGrath's final wish was granted, briefly. His body was returned to Souris, and he was indeed buried next to his wife. Short afterward, however, her body was disinterred and she was reburied two hundred kilometers away from the man who loved her too much to let her live.

James McGrath remains buried in the Souris cemetery. ✦

# 1902
## WALTER GORDON

Although July 20th, 1902 was an unusually cold morning in Brandon, the main topic of conversation in the city was not the weather. Uppermost was the execution of the man convicted of killing two area farmers a couple of years earlier. Walter Gordon was only twenty-three when he arrived in the province from Whitby, Ontario, and just a year older when he met the first of the men he was to murder.

After working for a year as a farm labourer Gordon entered into an agreement to purchase the Boissevain farm of Charles Daw. When the money to complete the transaction was not forthcoming Daw confronted Gordon and the discussion quickly became heated. It was brought to an abrupt end, however, when Gordon suddenly drew his revolver and shot Daw. A few days later a friend of the murdered farmer showed up at the Daw farm to inquire about his friend's whereabouts. When it became obvious that he was not convinced by Gordon's explanations he became the murderer's second victim, and his body joined that of Daw at the bottom of a nearby well.

Friends of the missing men eventually became concerned and one contacted the authorities about his suspicions. When the police arrived in the area to investigate a neighbour of Daw recalled that Daw's dog had been acting strangely about the time of the farmer's disappearance, particularly around an abandoned well. That comment led to the discovery not only of the bodies of the missing men, but of the dog as well.

News of the murders quickly spread and wanted posters were distributed throughout Canada and the United States. When Gordon was recognized in South Dakota he promptly returned to Canada where he joined a regiment on its way to fight in the Boer War. He was arrested in Halifax just hours before his unit was to board ship for South Africa.

The morning Gordon was to hang dawned cold and overcast. At 6:00 am the wife of the governor of the Brandon Jail delivered the condemned man his last meal. Gordon politely thanked her, declined the food, but said that he would welcome a cup of tea. Two hours later the 150 spectators who managed to obtain tickets to the execution saw the jail door open and the condemned man approach the scaffold. As the prisoner stepped onto the trap door he was asked if he had any last words. When Gordon shook his

> Rather than being interred within the walls of the place were he was executed, his body was quietly released to his mother and father and buried in an unmarked grave in what at the time was a Roman Catholic cemetery.

head a black hood was quickly pulled over his face. Eighteen minutes elapsed from the time the trap sprung until he was declared dead.

Walter Gordon is unique among those hanged in Canada. Rather than being interred within the walls of the place were he was executed, his body was quietly released to his mother and father and buried in an unmarked grave in what at the time was a Roman Catholic cemetery. Two years later his mother arranged to have a modest grave marker erected. Bearing only the initials "W.G.", it continues to bear stark tribute to one of western Manitoba's few serial killers.

Walter Gordon is buried in the Brandon cemetery. ✦

# 1888

# WILLIAM WEBB

On 1 September 1888 an abusive husband murdered his wife in front of the couple's four children. Four months later he became the first person to be hanged in Brandon, a city then barely six years old.

According to newspaper accounts, William Webb was working as a bank clerk in England when he met his future wife. After living for a time in England, the two immigrated to Canada. Although initially settled in Oak Lake, in 1881 they moved to Brandon, where they started Pacific Laundry.

The Webbs and their four children lived on the outskirts of Brandon, a little east of First Street and just south of Rosser Avenue. Attached to their small one-story house was a lean-to, out of which they conducted laundry business. William did the washing, his wife ironed, and their son delivered the finished product throughout the city with a wagon and pair of dogs.

Prior to the incident that resulted in the death of his wife Webb had regularly beaten her, and in 1886 even shot at her with a revolver. Although he missed, he was arrested and jailed. When Mrs. Webb refused to press charges against her husband, he was released.

• Justice T.W. Taylor

Leaving his horrified children standing over their mother's body, Webb rushed to the police station, where he confessed to the killing and asked to be arrested.

September 1st, 1888 was a Saturday. The Webbs had been working, and drinking, in their laundry for most of the day. According to evidence Webb gave at trial, the two had been unhappy for most of the sixteen or seventeen years of their marriage. On the day of the murder they had quarreled all morning, and when Mrs. Webb left the lean-to to fetch some sheets from a clothes line, still scolding him as she walked out, he had had enough.

Webb took a 12-gauge cartridge from a box and loaded a shotgun which had been leaning against a wall. Although he put the gun down when his wife re-entered the laundry, she was still taunting him; he picked it up again and, without aiming, shot her. The slug left a wound measuring about two by three inches, severing her carotid arteries and shattering her jaw. Leaving his horrified children standing over their mother's body, Webb rushed to the police station, where he confessed to the killing and asked to be arrested.

The coroner's inquest, held two days later, meant that her body remained where it fell, lying in a pool of blood and partly hidden under the table on which she had been ironing clothes. According to the *Brandon Sun,* over the weekend the scene attracted 'a great many' Brandon residents.

At trial Webb confessed to murdering his wife, and Chief Justice Thomas Wardlaw Taylor had no alternative but to sentence him to death. After urging the convicted man to seek pardon from an offended God, the judge ordered that Webb be removed to the common jail of the western judicial district and on December 28th be hanged within its walls.

In the days preceding his execution Webb watched impassively from his cell window as first his gallows was constructed and then his grave was dug. Even on the morning of his execution he appeared to take only a limited interest in what was going on as he sat on his bed, patiently awaiting imminent death.

A few minutes before 8:00 am a small group of men arrived at his cell. At a signal from the sheriff the executioner, wearing a mask and dressed in a fur coat, stepped forward. Without the slightest hesitation Webb placed his hands in front of him and stood expressionless as his wrists were pinioned to the leather belt strapped to his waist. The procession then left his cell. Just before it reached the gallows it re-formed so that the sheriff led the way up the steps of the scaffold, followed by the jail governor, the condemned man, his minister, the executioner and a guard.

As Webb stepped onto the trap door of the gallows it shifted slightly under his weight. Although momentarily startled, he regained composure and stood quietly as his

• Brandon Gaol

legs were strapped together, and then dutifully knelt so that a black hood and noose could be placed over his head.

As Webb started to repeat the Lord's Prayer the executioner stepped to his front and left and stood beside the lever which worked the trap doors. When the condemned man got to the phrase "and deliver us from all evil" the trap sprung. According to witnesses, when Webb reached the end of his eight foot drop all that could be seen was a quivering motion and a slight twitching of his limbs. Eighteen minutes later the abusive husband of Mary Jane Webb was declared dead.

William Webb was the fourth person to be hanged in Manitoba, and the first of four to be executed in Brandon. His remains are still buried in a corner of a small patio area just east of where the old Brandon jail once stood. His wife is believed to lie in an unmarked grave in the Brandon cemetery. ✦

# 1907

# LAWRENCE GOWLAND

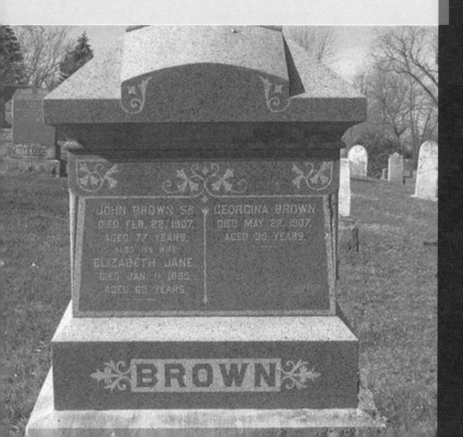

The last time John Brown saw his thirty-five-year-old sister alive she was in her bedroom getting dressed. The two worked a farm three miles east of Killarney that until the previous winter had been owned by their father. John was apprehensive about leaving his sister alone with their hired man, and before leaving for town asked if she would be okay. Assured that she was fine, he left.

Ten minutes later the twenty-year old subject of John's concern came in from the veranda and walked upstairs to his room. He removed his boots and socks, picked up his straight razor, and walked out. Georgina Brown was standing in front of her bedroom window, probably watching her brother recede into the distance, when Lawrence Gowland crept in. Before she sensed his presence he dragged her to the floor.

For a moment Brown actually had the upper hand, wrenching the razor from her attacker. Her grip was not strong, however, and he wrestled it back. Even though Gowland confessed, he refused to say whether he raped her and then cut her throat from ear to ear, or killed her before the assault.

In either case, Gowland left Brown lying in a pool of blood and walked to an adjoining room, where he rolled two cigarettes. He then returned to his victim's bedroom and smoked them as he periodically parted her curtains to see if anyone was approaching. Satisfied that he was alone, Gowland retreated to his own room, where he laid out his best clothes.

He next went downstairs in search of his employer's razor, having broken his own during his struggle with Georgina. When he could not find it, he took a butcher knife from the kitchen and made his way back upstairs. Standing beside his bed, he started to cut his own throat. After cutting into his windpipe, however, he decided to finish committing suicide while lying on his bed.

When John Brown rode into his yard he had been away three hours. He immediately noticed that Gowland had not taken out the horses, and he rushed into the house to find out why. Instead of an explanation he found his hired man unconscious, his throat cut. Worried about his sister, Brown quickly set off for his neighbour's farm, where she was to have spent the afternoon.

As soon as he was informed that Georgina had never arrived Brown returned home, to the mutilated body of his sister and the still unconscious Gowland.

• Morden Gaol

A week later the preliminary hearing looking into the murder of Georgina Brown was convened in the hospital room of her killer. Two of the first three witnesses testified that Gowland had admitted killing and brutalizing Brown. Gowland refused to describe the sexual aspect of the attack, however, saying only that it was something about which he did not care to speak.

The murder trial of Lawrence Gowland was held in Morden, the centre of the Killarney judicial district. By the time the trial got underway local hotels were full. From beginning to end the hearing lasted barely two hours, partly because one of the first pieces of evidence introduced was Gowland's confession, and partly because the presiding judge refused to appoint a lawyer to defend the accused. The crown, he suggested, did not have $50 to hire a public defender.

His only regret, he said, was for his mother, who "will feel it worse than I do. She will also miss the little money I used to send to help support her, and I don't know how she will live now, as she had a great struggle before."

Throughout the hearing Gowland remained silent. When asked if he had anything to say, he said no, he had nothing to add to what had already been said by others. His response was likely the reason the jury took just ten minutes to return a guilty verdict. Ironically, as Gowland's death sentence was pronounced it was the judge, not the condemned man, who lost composure.

There are two versions of how Gowland spent the next six weeks. The minister who visited him daily said that the killer fully realized what awaited him and made no pretense of accepting his fate with equanimity. Hours spent in prayer did not bring peace. His nights were restless, and when sleep arrived it came late and did not last long.

And then there was Gowland's version. In a letter written the day before he was executed he said that he was eating and sleeping well. His only regret, he said, was for his mother, who "will feel it worse than I do. She will also miss the little money I used to send to help support her, and I don't know how she will live now, as she had a great struggle before."

On the day Gowland was hanged the only people interested in the event were the court officials responsible for the execution. The coroner had difficulty finding enough people to make up the jury required by law to view the body of someone executed.

Shortly before eight o'clock in the morning on Friday the 13th, Morden's sheriff walked to the front of Gowland's cell and asked him to step into the hallway. The prisoner stood and, with a guard on either side, walked the sixty-five feet separating his cell and the gallows.

At the top of the scaffold Gowland stood, head erect, listening to a Bible reading as the hangman prepared for what was to come. He was listening to the beginning of the Lord's Prayer when the trap lever pulled. Six minutes later he was dead.

Georgina Brown was killed on May 22nd, 1907 and is buried in the Killarney cemetery. Lawrence Gowland was tried for her murder exactly five months later and executed on December 13th. He is buried in the yard of the Morden jail. ◆

# 1927

# EARL "THE STRANGLER" NELSON

**E**arl "the Strangler" Nelson was one of North America's most prolific and earliest serial killers. In twenty months preceding his capture he was accused of murdering and sexually molesting more than twenty-six women. His record would likely have been worse had it not been for the actions of two Killarney area residents.

Nelson was born in San Francisco in 1897 and raised by maternal grandparents. Their puritanical fanaticism had a significantly negative influence on him, which became apparent in 1918 when he molested the twelve-year-old daughter of a San Francisco family. He was arrested, diagnosed as psychopathic, but discharged after numerous escape attempts started to have an impact on the mental hospital's budget.

The first murder attributed to Nelson was committed in Philadelphia in 1925. Within three weeks he strangled and sexually abused two more women. Almost immediately authorities noticed that a "Room for Rent" sign had been hanging in the window of each home, and that in each case clothing had been taken and later pawned.

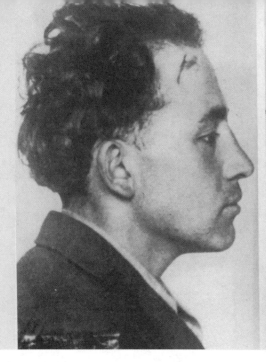
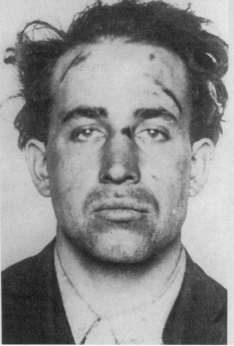

She found Nelson a hammer and asked him to start by repairing a screen door. As soon as the woman's back was turned, however, he attacked and strangled her.

Nelson's method next appeared in San Francisco. Between February and August 1926 five women were strangled and over the next six months other victims were discovered in Stockton, Portland, Seattle, Council Bluffs, Kansas City, Philadelphia, Buffalo, Detroit and Chicago. By the time Nelson reached Winnipeg in June 1927 he had already allegedly murdered twenty-four women.

According to evidence at trial, the Strangler was picked up at the Canada-US border by a Winnipeg couple who dropped him off at the corner of Corydon and Osborne. Nelson then made his way to Smith Street, where he noticed a "Room for Rent" sign in the window of the residence of Katherine Hill. Five hours later he was standing on the steps of the house when he was approached by Lola Gowan, a fourteen year old girl selling artificial flowers door-to-door.

He bought some and asked the young woman to follow him upstairs, where he said he had left his wallet. As soon as Gowan entered his room Nelson stunned her with a blow to her head and strangled her with a cloth. He then shoved her body under his bed.

The following morning the killer left with Gowan's belongings. Shortly before noon he noticed a "Room for Rent" sign in the window of the Riverton Avenue home of Emily Patterson. When Patterson answered the door Nelson asked if he could pay for renting a room by doing repair work around the house. Patterson agreed. She found Nelson a hammer and asked him to start by repairing a screen door. As soon as the woman's back was turned, however, he attacked and strangled her.

When Nelson completed his sexual ritual he changed into a suit belonging to the husband of the dead woman and walked to a nearby pawnshop, where he exchanged it for one his size. He then began hitch-hiking west. He got as far as Regina before noticing that every newspaper he read carried both his description and a description of the suit he was wearing. At a Regina pawnshop he once again exchanged his clothes, but this time an observant clerk noticed the Winnipeg labels and promptly phoned the police.

Nelson was not immediately captured because the owner of the car that picked him up was a scrap metal dealer who traveled east from Regina well off the highways patrolled by the police. The Strangler's luck, however, was about to run out. After catching several rides from Boissevain he ended up in Wakopa, a village located near Killarney five miles from the United States border. About 6 pm he bought food in a store owned by Leslie Morgan. Albert Dingwall, a Wakopa grain buyer, was entering the store as Nelson walked out. He recognized the fugitive, and he and Morgan briefly followed the killer as Mrs. Morgan phoned the Manitoba Provincial Police detachment in Killarney. Nelson was arrested without a struggle just as he was about to enter the United States.

In Killarney the Strangler was searched, placed in a cell in the basement of the town hall, and left alone while the detachment's only constable phoned a report of the capture to his superiors. Under his bed Nelson found an old nail file, and he promptly used it to pick the lock on his cell door. Intent on escaping to the United States, he made his way to the railway where he concealed himself in a nearby lumberyard. The first whistle that sounded the next morning brought Nelson from his hiding place. Ironically, the train was pulling a carload of policemen sent to help in the search for the escapee. Nelson was immediately noticed and arrested.

On 4 November 1927 it took a jury only forty-eight minutes to convict Earl Leonard Nelson of murdering Emily Patterson. Two months later he was hanged and his body was shipped by his wife to San Francisco for burial. ✦

# 1939

## MANITOBA'S ONLY TRIPLE HANGING

Eleven months after three Dauphin area men kicked eighty-one- year-old Anna Cottick to death. the killers earned two spots in the annals of Canadian crime. Their execution the only time in Manitoba history that three people were hanged for committing a single murder, and their secretly taped jail-house conversations were the first introduced in a provincial court.

On 14 May 1938 Peter Korzenowski, Dan Prytula and a friend consumed nearly 100 ounces of homebrew before deciding to rob Anna Cottick and her ninety-one year-old husband. Around midnight they roused a sleeping William Kanuka and insisted that he take them to his neighbour's farm.

When the men arrived Korzenowski and Prytula got out of Prytula's car, which Kanuka drove about two and a half miles down the road, where he waited to pick them up. Armed with two revolvers, Korzenowski and Prytula smashed the glass out of a ground-floor window of the tiny house, fired two shots into it, and then crawled in.

They were immediately confronted by Elko Cottick, whom Prytula attacked with a large flashlight. Korzenowski, meanwhile, rushed to an adjoining room, where Anna had been sleeping. After beating her unconscious with a black-jack he began kicking her, eventually breaking nine ribs. Korzenowski and Prytula then carried Elko out of the farm-house, but once outside seemed to change their mind and re-entered the tiny residence and threw the Cotticks down into a fruit cellar, where they were found the next morning by their grandson.

Rumours that the two elderly Fishing River district farmers kept more than $1,000 in their home proved untrue, and Anna's killers departed with only twenty-three dollars.

After leaving the Cottick farm Kanuka, Korzenowski and Prytula drove seven miles west, where they robbed and nearly beat to death another octogenarian farmer. Part way through that assault one of them noticed that the sun was beginning to rise and told his companions that it was time to go.

Within twenty-four hours all three were arrested, turned in by a friend who was with them during the two break-ins but not charged with taking part in the beatings. The process of finding enough corroborating evidence to obtain murder convictions was the stuff of modern crime dramas.

As soon as the Royal Canadian Mounted Police arrived at the Cottick farm, members noticed fresh tire tracks entering and leaving the yard. They were tracked three miles west to within 150 yards of Kanuka's residence, and from there to the Gilbert Plains home of Prytula's sister. The tire marks were a perfect match to the treads on Prytula's 1929 Ford. It was confiscated and, while casts were taken of its treads, Prytula was arrested and his blood-stained clothes, boots and three .32 calibre bullets were seized and sent to the RCMP crime lab for testing.

As one group of police officers were arresting Prytula and Korzenowski, another searched the Cottick residence for additional evidence. Almost immediately they noticed what appeared to be fingerprints on the glass smashed by the assailants. Fragments were sent to experts in Winnipeg, along with a window frame and piece of wall where the bullets fired by Korzenkowski and Prytula lodged.

The RCMP also searched the residence and yard of Korzenowski, located a few hundred yards from where Kanuka had been staying. There they found the revolvers used in the break-ins, hidden in a pile of stones. Korzenowski was promptly arrested, and three days later he and his two friends were part of an identification line-up paraded in front of the hospital beds of the Cotticks.

While the police were waiting for results of forensic tests being carried out in Dauphin, Regina and Winnipeg, they held the alleged killers on a coroner's warrant. That changed on June 1st, when the three were formally charged with murder. The proceeding seemed to amuse Kanuka, who entered and left the courtroom with a broad grin on his face.

His amusement turned to stern concern, however, when he learned that conversations between him and his co-accused were recorded by a dictagraph placed in the ventilators and registers of their cells.

When those recordings were introduced at trial it became clear that the men were shocked at the amount of scientific evidence gathered by the police. On one occasion an obviously perplexed Prytula was heard complaining that despite eight years experience robbing people, "I got caught with the tires. I do not understand it." Another complaint was the cost of his lawyer. "No wonder one has to go robbing."

A combination of eyewitness testimony, scientific evidence and their own words sealed their fate. After a week-long trial and four hours of deliberation a Dauphin jury found them guilty of murder. Kanuka was the only one to receive a recommendation for mercy, and the only one to react to the verdict. "I did not enter the house, and I killed no one, and I do not think I should hang."

Only once previously had a Manitoba court sentenced three people to hang for taking part in a single murder. In 1918 three men were condemned to death for taking the life of a Winnipeg police officer, but the sentence of the youngest was commuted to life imprisonment.

Korzenowski and Kanuka were hanged side-by-side in the Headingley Gaol just after midnight on Thursday, 16 February 1939. While life slowly ebbed out of them Prytula waited his turn, but not for long. It took jail officials exactly fourteen minutes to take down the bodies of Kanuka and Korzenowski and spring the trap on Prytula, five minutes longer than it took him to die.

None of the bodies were claimed, and for nearly forty years they were interred in Headingley Gaol. In the mid-1970s, however, theirs and the bodies of twelve other executed men were disinterred and moved to a small plot of land a mile west of the jail. ✦

# bibliography

**CHAPTER ONE: PIONEERS**

1.  William Henry (Squire) Sowden
    (a) Archival material, Souris Museum.
    (b) Brown, Alice E., "Early Days in Souris and Glenwood" (1953-54) 10 *MHS Transactions,* Series 3 at 30; and at www.mhs.mb.ca/docs/transactions/3/sourisglenwood.shtml
    (c) Sanqwine, Mrs. V.H., "Stroll Across Our Swinging Bridge" (April, 1957) *Manitoba Pageant*; and at www.mhs.mb.ca/docs/pageant/02/swingingbridge.shtml.
    (d) Souris & District Heritage Club, Inc., *The People of Souris and Glenwood: From the Earliest Beginnings to the Present* (Souris: Souris & District Heritage Club, Inc., 2006).
    (e) Stevenson, Lorraine, "A bridge to the future" in (9 December 2004) *Farmers' Independent Weekly* 35.
    (f) Tyman, John Langton, *By Section, Township & Range: Studies in Prairie Settlement,* 2nd (Brandon: Brandon University, 1995) 94.

2.  Charles Arkoll Boulton
    (a) Boulton, Major Charles A., *Reminiscences of the North-West Rebellions* (Toronto: Grip,1886) and at wsb.datapro.net/rebellions/index.html
    (b) Boulton, Charles Arkoll & Heather Robertson, ed., *I Fought Riel: A Military Memoir* (Toronto: James Lorimer, 1985).
    (c) Boulton, Mrs. Charles A., "Charles Arkall Boulton" in Family History, Town of Russell at www.russellmb.com/history/families/boulton.html
    (d) "Boulton, The Hon. Charles Arkel" in Parliament of Canada, Senators and Members, Senators, Historical at www.parl.gc.ca/common/SenatorsMemebers_senate
    (e) Coates, Ken, "Western Manitoba and the 1885 Rebellion" (1990) 20 *Manitoba History* 32; and at www.mhs.mb.ca/docs/mb_history/10/1885rebellion.shtml
    (f) Coates, Kenneth and Swan, Ruth, "Charles Arkoll Boulton" in Francess G. Halpenny & Jean Hamelin, eds., *Dictionary of Canadian Biography,* vol. 12 (Toronto: University of Toronto Press, 1990) 119; and at www.biographi.ca
    (g) Kempthorne, Roberta, "Behind Every Hero" (1992) 23 *Manitoba History* 23; and at www.mhs.mb.ca/docs/mb_history/23/behindeveryhero.shtml
    (h) "Louis Riel: Thomas Scott" in *The Heritage Centre* at www.shsb.mb.ca/Riel/escott.htm
    (i) "Perpetuated Unit: Boulton's Mounted Infantry — 1885" in The Fort Garry Horse at www.fortgarryhorse.ca

3.  Abraham Klenman
    (a) Archival materials, Jewish Heritage Centre of Western Canada.
    (b) Feldman, Anna, "Jewish Rural Settlements" in *The Encyclopedia of Saskatchewan* (Regina: Canadian Plains Research Center, 2005) 491; and at esask.uregina.ca
    (c) Gutkin, Harry, *Journey into Our Heritage; The Story of the Jewish People in the Canadian West* (Toronto: Lester & Orpen Dennys).
    (d) Lamm, Maurice, *The Jewish Way in Death and Mourning* (Jonathan David, New York, 1969).
    (e) Leonoff, Cyril Edel, *Wapella Farm Settlement: The First Successful Jewish Farm Settlement in Canada* (Winnipeg: Jewish Historical Society of Western Canada, 1972).
    (f) Menachemson, Nolan, *A Practical Guide to Jewish Cemeteries* at www.avotaynu.com/books/Cemeteries.htm
    (g) Trachtenberg, Henry, "Klenman, Abraham" in Ramsay Cook & Jean Hamelin, eds., *Dictionary of Canadian Biography*, vol. 13 (Toronto: University of Toronto Press, 1994) 556; and at www.biographi.ca.

4.  Adam (the 'fabulous Scot') McKenzie
    (a) McKenzie, A.F. (Dick), "The Fabulous Scot" (1959) 5:1 *Manitoba Pageant* and at www.mhs.mb.ca/docs/pageant/05/fabulousscot.shtml
    (b) Richards, Irene Lawrence, "The Story of Beautiful Plains" (1951-52) 8 *MHS Transactions,* Series 3 at 15; and at www.mhs.mb.ca/docs/transactions/3/beautifulplains.shtml.

5.  Chief One-Arrow
    (a) "Native Chief's Remains Return to Sask. Century After His Death" at www.cbc.ca/canada/manitoba/story/2007/08/24/one-arrow.html
    (b) Tyler, Kenneth J., "Kupeyakwuskonam, One Arrow" in Francess G. Halpenny & Jean Hamelin, eds., *Dictionary of Canadian Biography,* vol. 11 (Toronto: University of Toronto Press, 1982) 461; and at www.biographi.ca

6.  Dr. Frederick Valentine Bird
    (a) Archival material, Boissevain Community Archives.
    (b) Boissevain History Committee, *Beckoning Hills Revisited* (Boissevain: Boissevain History Committee, 1981).
    (c) "Dr. Frederick Valentine Bird" in Manitoba Agricultural Hall of Fame" at www.mts.net/~agrifame/bird.html

(d) McCallum, Gail, "Historical Tour — Boissevain, Manitoba" (1990) 20 *Manitoba History* 25; and at www.mhs.mb.ca/docs/mb_history/20/boissevain.shtml

7. Dr. Robert Stirton Thornton
(a) "The Doctor": Robert Stirton Thornton" in *Deloraine Scans A Century: A History of Deloraine and District, 1880-1980* (Deloraine: Deloraine History Book Committee, 1980) 703.
(b) *"Thornton, Robert Stirton M.D." in Legislative Assembly of Manitoba* at www.gov.mb.ca/legislature/members/bios_deceased.html

8. Eleanor Eliza Cripps (Kennedy)
(a) Fast, Vera K., "Cripps, Eleanor Eliza" in Ramsay Cook & Jean Hamelin, eds., *Dictionary of Canadian Biography,* vol. 14 (Toronto: University of Toronto Press, 1998) 251; and at www.biographi.ca
(b) "Kennedy, Eleanor E. (Cripps)" in *Pioneers and Early Citizens of Manitoba* (Winnipeg: Manitoba Library Association, 1971) 112.
(c) Shaw, Dr. E.C., "The Kennedys — An Unusual Western Family" (1972-73) 29 *MHS Transactions,* Series 3 at 69; and at www.mhs.mb.ca/docs/transactions/3/kennedys.shtml.
(d) Shaw, Edward C., M.D., "Captain William Kennedy, An Extraordinary Canadian" in (1970-71) 27 *MHS Transactions,* Series 3 at 7; and at www.mhs.mb.ca/docs/transactions/3/kennedy_w.shtml
(e) "William Kennedy" in Buy Orkney at www.buyorkney.com/roots/biographies/william_kennedy/

9. Charles Sankey
(a) Archival material, Waskada Museum.
(b) Brenda History Committee, *Bridging Brenda: Napinka, Medora, Waskada, Goodlands,* vols. 1& 2 (Waskada: Brenda History Committee, 1990).
(c) "Cutty Sark: the world's last tea clipper" at www.cuttysark.org.uk
(d) McVeigh, Karen, "Blaze ravages historic Cutty Sark" in *Globe and Mail,* Tuesday, 22 May 2007, p. A3.
(e) "The Ship Cutty Sark" at www.sankey.ws/cuttysark.html

**CHAPTER TWO: POLITICS**

10. John Andrew Davidson
(a) *Brandon Weekly Sun,* Thursday 19 November 1903, p. 1.
(b) *Manitoba Free Press,* Monday 16 November 1903, p. 11.
(c) *Manitoba Free Press,* Wednesday 18 November 1903, p. 6.
(d) Wendy Owen, "John Andrew Davidson" in *Ramsay Cook & Jean Hamelin,* eds., *Dictionary of Canadian Biography,* vol. 13 (Toronto: University of Toronto Press, 1994) 242; and at www.biographi.ca
(e) The Legislative Assembly of Manitoba, "John Andrew Davidson" at www.gov.mb.ca/legislature/members/bios_deceased.html

11. Harry William Cater
(a) *Brandon Daily Sun,* 13 November 1919, p. 1.
(b) Dr. W. Leland Clark, "Harry Cater: The Personification of the Successful Municipal Politician?" (1978-79) *35 MHS Transactions,* Series 3 at 49; and at www.mhs.mb.ca/docs/transactions/3/cater_h.shtml
(c) "Mayors of Brandon" in www.brandon.ca.nsf

12. Francis Evans Cornish
(a) Begg, Alexander & Nursey, Walter R., *Ten Years In Winnipeg: A Narration of the Principal Events in the History of the City of Winnipeg From the Year A.D. 1870 to the Year A.D. 1879,* Inclusive (Winnipeg: Times Printing, 1879).
(b) Burchill, John, "An Un-Auspicious Beginning" in *Winnipeg Police Service, History & Museum,* Historical Stories at www.winnipeg.ca/police/History/stories.stm
(c) Cemeteries Branch, "Francis Evans Cornish" in *125 Years, Brookside Cemetery, A Celebration of Life, Volume 1 — 1878-2003* (Winnipeg: City of Winnipeg, 2003) 61.
(d) "Francis Evans Cornish: London's First Native Born Mayor" at www.londonhistory.org
(e) Hartwell Bowsfield, "Francis Evans Cornish" in Marc La Terreur, ed., *Dictionary of Canadian Biography,* vol.10 (Toronto: University of Toronto Press, 1972) 197; and atwww.biographi.ca
(f) Rannie, Ruth Swan, "Frank Cornish — The Man" (1985) 9 *Manitoba History* 29; and at www.mhs.mb.ca/docs/mb_history/09/cornish_f.shtml

13. Stanley William McInnis
(a) *Brandon Weekly Sun,* Thursday 7 November 1907, p. 1, 2, 4.
(b) Clark, W. Leland, *Brandon's Politics and Politicians* (Brandon: Brandon Sun, 1981).
(c) *Manitoba Free Press,* Saturday 2 November 1907, p. 2.
(d) *Manitoba Free Press,* Monday 4 November 1907, p. 1.
(e) *Manitoba Free Press,* Tuesday 5 November 1907, p. 1.
(f) *Manitoba Free Press,* Wednesday 6 November 1907, p. 10.
(g) *Manitoba Free Press,* Friday 8 November 1907, p. 9.
(h) Mayba, I.I., "Stanley William McInnis" in Ramsay Cook & Jean Hamelin, eds., *Dictionary of Canadian Biography,* vol. 13 (Toronto: University of Toronto Press, 1994) 649; and at www.biographi.ca
(i) "Stanley William McInnis" in Legislative Assembly of Manitoba, at www.gov.mb.ca/legislature/members/bios_deceased.html.

14. Thomas Mayne Daly
(a) "Brandon (1908/10/26)" re Hon. Thomas Mayne Daly in *History of the Federal Electoral Ridings, 1867-1980,* vol. 1 (Ottawa: Library of Parliament, 1982) MA-2; and at www.gov.gc.ca/information/about/process/house.
(b) *Brandon Weekly Sun,* Thursday 29 June 1911, p. 2, 3.

(c) Daly, T. Mayne, *Canadian Criminal Procedure As the Same Relates to Summary Convictions and Summary Trials, With An Appendix of Forms* (Toronto: Carswell, 1911).

(d) Daly, T. Mayne, *A Treatise On the Winnipeg Juvenile Detention Home* (Toronto: Salvation Army Printing House, 1909).

(e) Daly, T. Mayne, *Canadian Immigration: Report On His Visit to Great Britain and Ireland, 1896* (Ottawa: G.P.O., 1896).

(f) "Daly, The Hon. Thomas Mayne, P.C." in Parliament of Canada, Senators and Members, House of Commons, Historical at www.parl.gc.ca/common/indx

(g) "Daly, Thomas Mayne" in Parliament of Canada, Senators and Members, House of Commons, Historical at www.parl.gc.ca/common/index

(h) Historic Resources Branch, *Thomas Mayne Daly* (Winnipeg: Department of Cultural Affairs & Historical Resources, 1982).

(i) Kendle, John, "Thomas Mayne Daly" in *Ramsay Cook & Jean Hamelin, eds., Dictionary of Canadian Biography,* vol. 14 (Toronto: University of Toronto Press, 1998) 265; and at www.biographi.ca

(j) *Manitoba Free Press,* 26 June 1911, p. 13.

(k) Members of the Orange Order, Grand Lodge Officers at www.ontorangewest.ca

(l) Patterson, George, ed., *Canadian Criminal Procedure As the Same Relates to Preliminary Hearings, Summary Convictions and Summary Trials, With An Appendix of Forms,* compiled by *the Hon. T.Mayne Daly,* 2nd (Toronto: Carswell, 1915).

(m) "Perth North (1872/02/20)" re Thomas Mayne Daly in *History of the Federal Electoral Ridiings, 1867-1980,* vol. 2 (Ottawa: Library of Parliament, 1982) 599; and at www.gov.gc.ca/information/about/process/house .

(n) Popple, A. E., ed., *Daly's Canadian Criminal Procedure and Practice Before Magistrates: Preliminary Hearings, Summary Convictions, Summary Trials, Speedy Trials, Trials By Jury and Criminal Appeals,* 3rd (Toronto: Carswell, 1936).

(o) "Selkirk (1887/02/22)" re Thomas Mayane Daly in *History of the Federal Electoral Ridings, 1867-1980,* vol. 1 (Ottawa: Library of Parliament, 1982) MA-98; and at www.gov.gc.ca/information/about/process/house

(p) "Selkirk (1892/11/02) By-Election)" *ibid.*

(q) "Sixth Ministry" at Government of Canada Privy Council Office at www.pco-bcp.gc.ca.

(r) "Stratford — Our City Life — Cemetery History" at www.stratford.on.ca

(s) "Stratford — Our City Life — Cemetery Search" at www.stratford.on.ca

(t) Stubbs, Roy St. George, "The First Juvenile Court Judge: The Honourable Thomas Mayne Daly KC" (1977-78) *34 MHS Transactions,* Series 3 at 49; and at www.mhs.mb.ca/docs/transactions/3/daly_tm.shtml

(u) "The Daly Family Tree" at www.mts.net

(v) "Thomas Mayne Daly" in Legislative Assembly of Ontario at www.ontla.on.ca/web/members/members

(w) Wallace, W. Stewart, ed., "Thomas Mayne Daly" in *Encyclopedia of Canada,* vol. II (Toronto: University Associates of Canada, 1948) 177.

15. Sir Clifford Sifton
(a) "Brandon (1896/11/27) (By-Election)" re Hon. Clifford Sifton in *History of the Federal Electoral Ridings,* 1867-1980, vol. 1 (Ottawa: Library of Parliament, 1982) MA-1; and at www.gov.ca/information/about/process/house

(b) "Brandon (1900/11/07)" *ibid.*

(c) "Brandon (1904/11/03)" *ibid.* at MA-2.

(d) "Brandon (1908/10/26)" *ibid.*

(e) Dafoe, John Wesley, *Clifford Sifton In Relation to His Times* (Toronto: Macmillan, 1931).

(f) "Eighth Ministry" in Government of Canada Privy Council Office at www.pco-bcp.gc.ca

(g) Hall, David J., "Sir. Clifford Sifton" in Ramsay Cook & Real Belanger, eds., *Dictionary of Canadian Biography,* vol. 15 (Toronto: University of Toronto Press, 2005) 941; and atwww.biographi.ca

(h) Hall, David J., *The Young Napoleon, 1861-1900,* vol. 1 (Vancouver: University of British Columbia Press, 1981).

(i) Hall, David J., *A Lonely Eminence, 1901-1929,* vol. 2 (Vancouver: University of British Columbia Press, 1981).

(j) *Manitoba Free Press,* Thursday 18 April 1929, p. 1.

(k) *Manitoba Free Press,* Friday 19 April 1929, p. 1.

(l) *Manitoba Free Press,* Monday 22 April 1929, p. 1.

(m) "Sifton, Clifford" in Legislative Assembly of Manitoba at www.gov.mb.ca/legislature/members/bios_deceased.html

(n) "Sifton, The Hon. Sir Clifford, P.C." in Parliament of Canada, Senators and Members, House of Commons, Historical at www.parl.gc.ca/common/index

(o) Truss, Jan, *The Judgment of Clifford Sifton: A Play* (Toronto: Playwrights Co-Op, 1979).

## CHAPTER THREE: ARTS & LEISURE

16. Francis Eugene Chaplin
(a) *Brandon Sun,* Thursday 3 December 1993, p. 1.

(b) *Brandon Sun,* Monday 6 December 1993, p. 8.

(c) "Brandon University School of Music" at www.brandonu.ca/Music/

(d) "CBC Television Series 1952 to 1982" at www.film.queensu.ca/CBC/Rec.html

(e) "Ehnes, James" in *Encyclopedia of Music in Canada*, 2nd (Toronto: University of Toronto Press, 1992).

(f) Jones, Lawrence, "Ehnes, Alan" in Helmut Kallmann & Gilles Potvin, eds., *Encyclopedia of Music in Canada,* 2nd (Toronto: University of Toronto Press, 1992) 409.

(g) "Maria Guidos-Albert" in *Timmins Symphony Orchestra* at www.timsym.com.

(h) Nichols, Kenneth, "Brandon University Trio" in *Helmut Kallmann & Gilles Potvin,* eds., *Encyclopedia of Music in Canada*, 2nd (Toronto: University of Toronto Press, 1992) 152. http://www.thecanadianencyclopedia.com/index
(i) Nichols, Kenneth & King, Betty Nygaard, "Chaplin, Francis (Eugene)" in *Helmut Kallmann & Gilles Potvin,* eds., *Encyclopedia of Music in Canada,* 2nd (Toronto: University of Toronto Press, 1992) 249.

(j) Spier, Susan, "Schultz, Victor" in *Helmut Kallmann & Gilles Potvin, eds., Encyclopedia of Music in Canada,* 2nd (Toronto: University of Toronto Press, 1992) 1201.http://www.thecanadianencyclopdeia.com/index(k) "Thomas Williams"in McGill Schulich School of Music, Department of Performance at www.mcgill.ca/thomas.williams.

17. James Freer

(a) Freer, Stan W., "Freer Family Genealogy Research — Canada" at www.home.cc.umanitoba.ca

(b) Kula, Sam, "Western Settlement and Steam Movies" (1985) *12:4 The Archivist 6*; and at www.collectionscanada.gc.ca/publications

(c) McKernan, Luke, "James S. Freer" in Stephen Herbert & Luke McKernan, eds., *Who's Who of Victorian Cinema: A Worldwide Survey* (London: BFI Publishing, 1996) 52; and at www.victorian-cinema.net/freer

(d) Morris, Peter, "Film History" in *The Canadian Encyclopedia,* 2nd , vol. 2 (Edmonton: Hurtig Publishers, 1988) 765; and at www.thecanadianencyclopedia.com/index

(e) Morris, Peter, *Embattled Shadows: a History of Canadian Cinema, 1895-1939*(Montreal: McGill-Queen's University Press, 1978).

(f) Walz, Gene, "100 Years of moviemaking" in *Winnipeg Real Estate News* (1997) 28 November 3.

(g) *Winnipeg Free Press,* 23 December 1933, 1, 9.

18. Paul Gerhardt Hiebert

(a) Besner, Neil, "Hiebert, Paul" in *The Canadian Encyclopedia,* 2nd , vol. 2 (Edmonton: Hurtig Publishers, 1988) 985; and at www.thecanadianencyclopedia.com/index

(b) Besner, Neil, "Sarah Binks" in *The Canadian Encyclopedia,* 2nd, vol. 3 (Edmonton: Hurtig Publishers, 1988) 1929; and at www.thecanadianencyclopedia.com/index

(c) Braun, Ernest, "Hiebert, Paul G. (1892-1987)" in Global Anabaptist Mennonite Encyclopedia Online, January 2005 at www.gameo.org.encyclcopedia/contents/

(d) Greer, John, *A Sarah Binks Songbook* (1988).

(e) Hiebert, Paul Gerhardt, *Sarah Binks* (Toronto: McClelland & Stewart, 1971).

(f) Macklin, Davis & Caron, Andrea, "Lost classics and guilty pleasures: Louise Penny on Sarah Binks" in 93:29 *The Manitoban* (12 April 2006) at The Manitoban Online at www.themanitoban.com/2005-2006.

(g) Noonan, Gerald A., "Incongruity and Nostalgia in Sarah Binks" (1978) 3.2 *Studies in Canadian Literature* at www.lib.unb.ca/Texts/SCL.

19. Frederick Philip Greve/Grove

(a) Hill, Colin, "Frederick Philip Grove (1879-1948)" in *The Literary Encyclopedia* (23 July 2004) at www.litencyc.com/php/speople

(b) Historic Resources Branch, *Frederick Philip Grove* (Winnipeg: Department of Cultural Affairs and Historical Resources, 1981).

(c) Lenoski, Daniel S., "Review Essay: Ronald A. Wells, ed., *Letters From a Young Emigrant in Manitoba: A Record of Emigrant Life in the Canadian West* (Winnipeg: University of Manitoba Press, 1981)" (1984) 7 *Manitoba History* 50; and at www.mhs.mb.ca/docs/mb_history/07/emigrantletters.shtml

(d) Mitchell, Ross, "Frederick Philip Grove, 1871-1948" in (1964) 10:1 *Manitoba Pageant* at www.mhs.mb.ca/docs/pageant/10/grove_fp.shtml

(e) Rapid City Historical Society, *Rapid City and District: Our Past For the Future* (Rapid City: Rapid City Historical Book Society, 1978).

(f) Spettigue, D.O., "Grove, Frederick Philip" in *The Canadian Encyclopedia,* 2nd, vol. 2 (Edmonton: Hurtig Publishers, 1988) 943; and at www.thecanadianencyclopedia.com/index

20. George Edwin Tackaberry

(a) Archival material, Daly House Museum.

(b) Ash, Bob, interview.

(c) *Brandon Sun,* 19 November 1937.

(d) Tackaberry, George, interview.

(e) *Winnipeg Free Press,* 9 December 1982.

21. Earl 'Sandy' Graham

(a) Cemeteries Branch, "Earl (Sandy) Graham" in *Brookside Cemetery: A Celebration of Life,* vol. 2 (Winnipeg: City of Winnipeg, 2003) 40.

(b) Cleaves, Slaid, "Quick as Dreams" in *Wishbones CD* (Philo Records, 2004).

(c) Hillenbrand, Laura, "A debt of remembrance" in (24 February 2001) Thoroughbred Times.com at www.thoroughbredtimes.com/commentary/2001/February/24/A-debt-of-remembrance.aspx

(d) Hillenbrand, Laura, *Seabiscuit, An American Legend* (New York: Random House Ballantine Publishing, 2001).

(e) "Jockeys' Guild History 1940-2000" in Jockeys' Guild at www.jockeysguild.com/history.php.

(f) Jockey's Guild, *The History of Race Riding and the Jockeys' Guild* (Nashville, Tenn.: Turner Publishing, 1998).

(g) "Seabiscuit, Famous Horses Biographies" in allhorseracing.com at www.allhorseracing.com/horse-racing/racebookhelp-famous-horses-seabiscuit.php.

22. Robert Harvey 'Bulldog' Brown

(a) "Bulldog" Bob Brown" in *Canadian Pro Wrestling Page of Fame* at www.garywill.com/wrestling/canada/brown

(b) "Bulldog Bob Brown" in Slam! Wrestling at www.canoe.ca/SlamWrestling/bulldogbrown

(c) " Bulldog" Bob Brown" in Wrestler Profiles, *Obsessed With Wrestling* at www.obsessedwithwrestling.com/profiles/b/bob-brown.

(d) Cemeteries Branch, "Robert Harold 'Bulldog' Brown" in *Brookside Cemetery: A Celebration of Life,* vol. 2 (Winnipeg: City of Winnipeg: 2003) 23.

(e) Murphy, Marli, "She Took the News of Bulldog's Death Hard" in *Kansas City Star,* 17 February 1997 at www.oldschool-wrestling.com/centralstateswrestling/Bob.

(f) Popper, Joe, "Bulldog Bob Brown: A Really Nice Tribute" in *Kansas City Star,* 1 March 1997 at www.oldschool-wrestling.com/centralstateswrestling/Bob

(g) Storm, Lance, "Bulldog Bob Brown" in StormWrestling.Com — commentary — August 23, 2004 at www.stormwrestling.com

**CHAPTER FOUR: CRIME**

23. Benito Murders

(a) Alvin Anderson, interview.

(b) Anderson, Frank, "Prairie Madness" *in Western Canadian Desperadoes: Little Known Tales of the Old West* (Saskatoon: Gopher Book No. 2, 1985, revised 1997) 27.

(c) "Constable George Campbell Harrison" in The Officer Down Memorial Page, Inc. at www.odmp.org/canada/officer/423-constable-george-campbell-harrison

(d) "Constable John George Shaw", ibid. at www.odmp.org/canada/officer/422-constable-john=george=shaw

(e) "Constable William Wainwright", ibid. at www.odmp.org/canada/officer/421-constable=william-wainwright

(f) "Doukhobors" in Religions in Canada at www.dnd.ca/hr/religions/engraph/religiions11

(g) "Doukhobor Stories and Articles" at www.doukhobor.org.stories

(h) Bill Fardoe, interview.

(i) "Sergeant Thomas Seller Wallace" in The Officer Down Memorial Page, Inc. at www.odmp.org/canada/officer/424-sergeant-thomas-seller-wallace.

(j) "Sgt. Thomas Wallace, Number 58 on the Honour Roll" at www.ucalgary.ca/~dsucha/mountie/wallace.

(k) Tarasoff, Koozma, "The Spirit Wrestlers, a website dedicated to The Doukhobors" at www.spirit-wrestlers.com

(l) Taylor, Scott, "Murder on the Prairies" in Winnipeg Police Service, History & Museum, Historical Stories at www.winnipeg.ca/police/History/story23

(m) "Wallace, Thomas S - SGT." in Last Post, RCMP Veteran's Association "Seven Dead in Police Fight: Crime Wave Takes Heavy Toll of Life" at www.rcmpveterans.com/wallace

(n) *Winnipeg Free Press,* 8 October 1935.

(o) *Winnipeg Free Press,* 9 October 1935.

(p) *Winnipeg Free Press,* 12 October 1935.

24. Lord Gordon Gordon

(a) Bovey, John A., "Gordon, Lord Gordon (alias Hon. Mr. Herbert Hamilton, Lord Glencairn, George Gordon, George Herbert Gordon, John Herbert Charles Gordon)" in Marc La Terreur, ed., *Dictionary of Canadian Biography,* vol. 10 (Toronto: University of Toronto Press, 1972) 307; and at www.biographi.ca

(b) Johnston, J.L., "Lord Gordon Gordon" (1950-51) 7 *MHS Transactions,* Series 3 at 7.

(c) *Manitoba Daily Free Press,* Monday 3 August 1874, p. 4.

(d) *Manitoba Daily Free Press,* Tuesday 4 August 1874.

(e) *Manitoba Daily Free Press,* Wednesday 5 August 1874, p. 2.

25. Lawrence Lees

(a) *Brandon Sun,* 15 July 1932.

(b) *Brandon Sun,* 16 July 1932.

(c) *Brandon Sun,* 18 July 1932.

(d) *Prairie Farmer,* 20 July 1932.

(e) Rossburn History Club, *On the Sunny Slopes of the Riding Mountains, a History of Rossburn and District* (Rossburn: Rossburn History Club, 1984).

(f) *Winnipeg Free Press,* 15 July 1932.

(g) *Winnipeg Free Press,* 19 July 1932.

(h) *Winnipeg Free Press,* 22 July 1932.

26. John Alexander Machray

(a) Blanchard, Jim, "The Machray Scandal" (1997) 33 *Manitoba History* 27; and at www.mhs.mb.ca/docs/mb_history/33/machrayscandal.shtml

(b) "Bad Bursars" in *Time Magazine,* 3 October 1932 at www.time.com/time/magazine/article

(c) Blanchard, Jim, "Great Defalcation: Machray didn't spend the money" in Letters to the Editor, 94:15 *Manitoban Oline* 29 November 2006 at www.themanitoban.com/2006-2007/1129/120. Letters.to.the.editor

(d) "Manitoba Lawyer" in *Time Magazine,* 5 September 1932 at www.time.com/time/magazine/article

(e) Vanderhart, Tessa, "The great defalcation" in 94:14 *Manitoban Online* 22 November 2006 at www.themanitoban.com/2006-2007/1122/114.The.great.defalcation

(f) *Winnipeg Free Press,* Saturday 24 September 1932, p. 1.

(g) *Winnipeg Free Press,* Friday 6 October 1933, p. 5.

(h) *Winnipeg Free Press,* Saturday 7 October 1933, p. 2.

27. Henry Roch Murder

(a) *Brandon Weekly Sun,* Thursday 26 October 1916, p. 5.

(b) *Brandon Weekly Sun,* Thursday 16 November 1916, p. 6.

(c) *Manitoba Free Press,* Wednesday 18 October 1916, p. 1.

(d) *Manitoba Free Press,* Thursday 19 October 1916, p. 1.

(e) *Manitoba Free Press,* Friday 20 October 1916, p. 4.

(f) *Manitoba Free Press,* Tuesday 24 October 1916, p. 3.

(g) *Manitoba Free Press,* Saturday 28 October 1916, p. 13.

(h) *Manitoba Free Press,* Friday 17 November 1916, p. 5.

(i) *Manitoba Free Press,* Friday 24 November 1916.

(j) *Manitoba Free Press,* Thursday 1 February 1917, p. 5.

(k) *Manitoba Free Press,* Saturday 3 February 1917, p. 4.

(l) *Manitoba Free Press,* Wednesday 20 June 1917, p. 5.

(m) *Manitoba Free Press,* Thursday 21 June 1917, p. 8.

(n) *Manitoba Free Press,* Saturday 23 June 1917, p. 3.

(o) *Manitoba Free Press,* Tuesday 26 June 1917, p. 8.

(p) *Manitoba Free Press,* Wednesday 27 June 1917, p. 5.

(q) *Manitoba Free Press,* Thursday 28 June 1917, p. 8.

(r) *Manitoba Free Press,* Friday 6 July 1917, p. 5.

(s) *Manitoba Free Press,* Friday 13 July 1917, p. 1.

(t) *Manitoba Free Press,* Thursday 4 October 1917, p. 4.

28. Sitar Family Massacre

(a) Holliday, Bob, "Devil's Hatchet Man" in *Winnipeg Sun,* Sunday 29 August 2004 at www.vinylrake.org/blogs/demon/2004/08/devils-hatchet-man.

(b) *Winnipeg Free Press,* Saturday 30 January 1932, p. 1.

(c) *Winnipeg Free Press,* Monday 1 February 1932, p. 1.

(d) *Winnipeg Free Press,* Tuesday 2 February 1932, p. 1.

(e) *Winnipeg Free Press,* Wednesday 3 February 1932, p. 1.

(f) *Winnipeg Free Press,* Friday 5 February 1932, p. 1.

(g) *Winnipeg Free Press,* Tuesday 22 March 1932, p. 1.

(h) *Winnipeg Free Press,* Wednesday 23 March 1932, p. 1.

(i) *Winnipeg Free Press,* Thursday 24 March 1932, p. 10.

(j) *Winnipeg Free Press,* Tuesday 7 June 1932, p. 4.

29. George Robson Coldwell

(a) *Brandon Weekly Sun,* Thursday 21 November 1907, p. 3.

(b) *Brandon Weekly Sun,* Thursday 23 September 1915, p. 2, 15.

(c) *Brandon Weekly Sun,* Thursday 14 October 1915, p. 13.

(d) *Brandon Weekly Sun,* Thursday 6 April 1916, p. 9.

(e) *Brandon Weekly Sun,* Thursday 29 June 1916, p. 5.

(f) *Brandon Weekly Sun,* Thursday 7 September 1916, p. 1.

(g) *Brandon Daily Sun,* Tuesday 30 January 1917, p. 1.

(h) *Brandon Daily Sun,* Thursday 24 January 1924, p. 1.

(i) *Brandon Daily Sun,* Friday 25 January 1924, p. 1.

(j) *Brandon Daily Sun,* Monday 28 January 1924, p. 5.

(k) Clark, W. Leland, *Brandon's Politics and Politicians* (Brandon: Brandon Sun, 1981).

(l) "Coldwell, George Robson KC" in Legislative Assembly of Manitoba at www.gov.mb.ca/legislature/memebers/bios_deceased

(m) *Manitoba Free Press,* Thursday 26 August 1915, p. 1.

(n) *Manitoba Free Press,* Tuesday 31 August 1915, p. 5.

(o) *Manitoba Free Press,* Wednesday 1 September 1915, p. 1.

(p) *Manitoba Free Press,* Thursday 2 September 1915, p. 2.

(q) *Manitoba Free Press,* Saturday 4 September 1915, p. 3.

(r) *Manitoba Free Press,* Monday 6 September 1915, p. 5.

(s) *Manitoba Free Press,* Wednesday 8 September 1915, p. 5.

(t) *Manitoba Free Press,* Thursday 9 September 1915, p. 8.

(u) *Manitoba Free Press,* Monday 13 September 1915, p. 7.

(v) *Manitoba Free Press,* Tuesday 14 September 1915, p. 5.

(w) *Manitoba Free Press,* Wednesday 15 September 1915, p. 5.

(x) *Manitoba Free Press,* Thursday 16 September 1915, p. 1.

(y) *Manitoba Free Press,* Saturday 18 September 1915, p. 1.

(z) *Manitoba Free Press,* Tuesday 5 September 1916, p. 1.

(aa) *Manitoba Free Press,* Wednesday 6 September 1916.

(bb) *Manitoba Free Press,* Monday 30 October 1916, p. 1.

(cc) *Manitoba Free Press,* Tuesday 28 November 1916, p. 3.

(dd) *Manitoba Free Press,* Wednesday 20 June 1917.

(ee) *Manitoba Free Press,* Tuesday 26 June 1917, p. 1.

(ff) Morton, W.L., *Manitoba, A History* (Toronto: University of Toronto Press, 1957).

## CHAPTER FIVE: THE FORGOTTEN

30. Hugh Marshall Dyer

(a) Beaverbrook, William Maxwell Aitken, Baron, *Canada In Flanders, The Official Story of the Canadian Expeditionary Force,* vol. 1 (London: Hodder & Stoughton, 1917).

(b) Dyer, Bill & Viola, *Minnedosa Valley Views* (Winnipeg: Inter-Collegiate Press, 1982).

(c) Harvey, Dr. Robert, "General H.M. Dyer of Westhope" in *Brandon Sun,* 28 April 1962.

(d) Harvey, Dr. Robert, "Dyer of Westhope" in *Pioneers of Manitoba* (Winnipeg: Prairie Publishing, 1970) 1.

(e) "Hugh Marshall Dyer, Brigadier General" at www.geocities.com/val_james/genealogy/profiles/hugh_marshall_dyer

(f) "Lieutenant Colonel Hugh Marshall Dyer" in *Canadian Great War Project*, CEF Soldier Detail at www.canadiangreatwarproject.com/searches/soldierDetail.

(g) "Marquette" in *History of the Federal Electoral Ridings,* 1867-1980, vol. 1 (Ottawa: Library of Parliament, 1982) MA-48.http://www.parl.gc.ca/information/about/process/house/hfer

(h) *Regina Leader-Post,* Wednesday 28 December 1938, p. 1.

(i) Schofield, Frank Howard, *The Story of Manitoba* (Winnipeg: S.J. Clarke Co., 1913).

(j) *Winnipeg Tribune,* Tuesday 27 December 1938, p. 1.

31.  Paul Harvey Wolos

(a) "Casualties of War Canadians serving with the U.S. Marines" in Casualties Marines in VietNam — Canadians at www.marzone.com/7thMarines/Hst5001

(b) "Casualty Record for Paul Harvey Wolos" at www.no-qquarter.org/code/details

(c) "Wolos" in *Henderson's Brandon (Manitoba) City Directory 1965* (Winnipeg: Henderson Directories, 1965) 264; and 1966 at 297, 1967 at 305 and 1968 at 311.

(d) "In Memory of Private First Class Paul Harvey Wolos" at www.tanaya.net/cgi-bin/vmw

(e) Levant, Victor, *Quiet Complicity, Canadian Involvement in the Vietnam War* (Toronto: Between the Lines, 1986).

(f) Levant, Victor, "Vietnam War" at www.thecanadianencyclopedia.com/index

(g) "Operation Union" at Echo 2/3, United States Marine Corps, Combat Operations at www.echo23marines6569.org/Operations

(h) "Operation Union and Union II" at www.combatwife.net/unionIandII.

(i) "Paul Harvey Wolos 18E, 112" in Vietnam Veterans Memorial Fund at www.vvmf.org/index.cfm

(j) Taylor, Charles, *Snow Job: Canada, the United States, and Vietnam* (1954-1973) (Toronto: Anansi, 1975).

(k) "Vietnam War Statistics" at www.capmarine.com/cap/statistics

32.  Brandon Asylum For the Insane

(a) *Brandon Weekly Sun,* 10 November 1910, p. 1.

(b) McRae, James, Interview.

(c) Refvik, Kurt, *A Centennial History of the Brandon Asylum* (Brandon: Brandon Publishing, 1991).

(d) Refvik, Kurt, "Brandon Asylum Fire of 1910" (1991) 21 *Manitoba History* 17; and at www.mhs.mb.ca/docs/mb_history/21/brandonasylumfire.shtml

33.  Souris City

(a) McFadden, Clifford R., "Souris City" (1972) 17:3 Manitoba Pageant 15.

(b) Morton, W.L., *Manitoba, A History* (Toronto: University of Toronto Press, 1967).

(c) Mulligan, Helen & Ryder, Wanda, *Ghost Towns of Manitoba: A Record of Pioneer Life* (Winnipeg: Great Plains, 2003) 108.

(d) Wawanesa & District History Book Committee, *Sipiweske: Light Through the Trees, 100 Years of Wawanesa and District* (Wawanesa: Wawanesa & District History Book Committee, 1988).

## CHAPTER SIX: ACCIDENTS & DISASTERS

34.  Lewis Hickman

(a) Barczewski, Stephanie L., *Titanic: A Night Remembered* (London: Hambledon & London, 2004).

(b) Campbell, Karen, "Woebegone Museum" in Memphis Flyer at www.weeklywire.com/ww/10-12-98/memphis_trvl.html

(c) "Halifax and the Titanic Victims" at www.titanic.gov.ns.ca/graves.html

(d) Handmer, Alison, "Victim of Fate" in The University of Sydney at www.usyd.edu.au/about/publication/gazette/april03/features/pub/titanic.shtml

(e) "Mr. Ambrose Hood Jr" in Encyclopedia Titanic at www.encyclopedia-titanic.org/biography/459/

(f) "Mr. Leonard Mark Hickman" in Encyclopedia Titanic at www.encyclopedia-titanic.org/biography/448/

(g) "Mr. Lewis Hickman" in Encyclopedia Titanic at www.encyclopedia-titanic.org/biography/449/

(h) "Mr. Percy William Deacon" in Encyclopedia Titanic at www.encyclopedia-titanic.org/biography/395/

(i) "Mr. Stanley George Hickman" in Encyclopedia Titanic at www.encyclopedia-titanic.org/biography/450/

(j) "Mr. William Dibden" in Encyclopedia Titanic at www.encyclopedia-titanic.org/biography/399

(k) *Neepawa Press,* 3 May 1912.

(l) *Neepawa Press,* 7 May 1912.

(m) Pittman, Cecil, interview.

(n) "RMS Titanic: List of Bodies and Disposition of Same" in Public Archives of Nova Scotia at www.gov.ns.ca/nsarm/cap/titanic/list.asp?Letter=H.

(o) "RMS Titanic's Second Class Passenger List" at www.home.swipnet.se/maltez/maltez_passaeiros1C.htm

(p) "The Grave of the Titanic" in Gulf of Marine Aquarium at www.gma.org/space1/titanic.html

(q) "The Search For the Dead" in Titanic — A Voyage of Discovery at www.euronet.nl/users/keesree/dead.htm

(r) "Titanic" at www.halifax.ca/history/titanic.html.

(s) "Titanic FAQ Page" in Frequently asked Questions, Maritime Museum of the Atlantic at www.museum.gov.ns.ca/mma/research/titanicfaq.html

(t) *Winnipeg Sun,* 12 April 1998.

(u) Wormstedt, Bill, "An Analysis of the Bodies Recovered from the Titanic" at http://home.att.net/~wormstedt/titanic/analysis.html

35. The Manitoba Power Commission
(a) Bentley, L., interview.
(b) *Brandon Sun,* 14 September 1957.
(c) Bulletin, Manitoba Power commission, October, 1954.
(d) Lako, Jean, interview.
(e) Nelson, Ivan, interview.
(f) Power, Irv, interview.

36. Archibald L. McMillan
(a) Booth, Robert, "First Police Chief Archibald L. McMillan" [unpublished].
(b) *Brandon Sun,* Thursday 17 December 1885, p. 1.
(c) *Brandon Sun,* Thursday, 24 December 1885, p. 1.
(d) *Brandon Sun,* Thursday 11 February 1886.
(e) *Manitoba Daily Free Press,* Thursday 17 December 1885, p. 1.
(f) *Manitoba Daily Free Press,* Saturday 19 December 1885, p. 1.

37. Brandon Train Wreck
(a) *Brandon Sun,* 13 January 1916.
(b) Hollihan, Tony, *Disasters of Western Canada: Courage Amidst the Chaos* (Edmonton: Folklore Publishing, 2004) 207.

38. Lloyd Wesley Shields
(a) "A Bomb fell On an Open Air Dance" (Brandon: Daly House Museum).
(b) Archival materials, Commonwealth Air Training Plan Museum, Brandon, Manitoba.
(c) *Brandon Sun,* 16 July 1943.
(d) Fardoe, Bill, interview.
(e) Ferguson, Hugh, interview.
(f) Ferguson, Isabel, interview.

39. Olympia Restaurant Fire
(a) *Brandon Sun,* 7 April 1953.
    *Brandon Sun,* 8 April 1953.
(b) Hamilton, Jack, interview.
(c) Hume, Mary, ed., *Brandon: a prospect of a city* (Brandon: City of Brandon, 1982) 185.
(d) Mundell, Dub, interview.

40. Alexander Harvest Fire
(a) *Brandon Weekly Sun,* 16 September 1915.
(b) *Manitoba Free Press,* 13 September 1915.

41. William Curle
(a) *Brandon Weekly Sun,* 10 September 1903.
(b) Bray, Phylis, interview.
(c) Centennial Committee, *Homesteaders and Homemakers: A History of Elton Municipality in its First Century* (Brandon: Elton Historical Committee, 1973).
(d) Council records (4 September 1903), City of Brandon.
(e) Franklin, Lloyd, interview.

42. Louis Slotin
(a) Anderson, H.L., A. Novick and P. Morrison, "Louis A. Slotin: 1912-1946" in (1946) 104 Science 182.
(b) "Louis Slotin" in *Manitobans Who Made A Difference* (Winnipeg: Manitoba Heritage, Culture and Tourism, 2007) at www.gov.mb.ca/chc/hrb/events/famous_manitobans/slotin_l.html
(c) "Louis Slotin" in science.ca at www.science.ca/scientists/scientist-profile.
(d) Martin, Brigitt, "The Secret Life of Louis Slotin 1910-1946 in (1999) 59:3 *Alumni Journal of the University of Manitoba;* and at www.cns-snc.ca/history/pioneers/slotin/slotin.html        .
(e) *Winnipeg Free Press,* 16 April 1999, p. D1.
(f) Zeilig, Martin, "Louis Slotin and 'The Invisible Killer'" in (1995) 75:4 *The Beaver* 20; and at www.hhs55.com/slotin.html.

**CHAPTER SEVEN: EXECUTED**

43. Harry Green
(a) "Green, Harry" in Persons Sentenced to Death in Canada, 1876-1976: An Inventory of Case Files in the Fonds of the Department of Justice, 140 at data2.archives.ca/pdf/pdf001/p000001052.pdf.
(b) *Manitoba Free Press,* Wednesday 23 December 1914, p. 12.

44. Jack Krafchenko
(a) *Brandon Weekly Sun,* Thursday 11 December 1913, p. 7.
(b) Burchill, John, "Bloody Jack" in Winnipeg Police Service, History & Museum, Historical Stories at www.winnipeg.ca/police/History/story8.stm.
(c) Burchill, John, "At the End of the Rope" in *Winnipeg Police Service, History & Museum,* Historical Stories at www.winnipeg.ca/police/History/story27.stm
(d) Cemetery Branch, 1*25 Years: Brookside Cemetery, A Celebration of Life,* Volume 1 — 1878-2000 (Winnipeg: City of Winnipeg, 2003) 53.

(e)  Gray, James H., *The Boy From Winnipeg* (Toronto: Macmillan, 1970) 75.

(f)  "Krafchenko, John (alias Kraff; Ryan, Tommy)" in Persons Sentenced to Death in Canada, 1876-1976: An inventory of Case Files in the Fonds of the Department of Justice 176 at data2.archives.ca/pdf/pdf001/p000001052.pdf

(g)  *Manitoba Free Press,* Thursday 4 December 1913, p. 1.

(h)  *Manitoba Free Press,* Friday 5 December 1913, p. 1.

(i)  *Manitoba Free Press,* Saturday 6 December 1913, p. 15.

(j)  *Rex v. Krafchenko,* (1914), 28 W.L.R. 76, 24 Man. R. 652, (22) C.C.C. 277, 17 D.L.R. 244 [K.B.].

(k)  Zeilig, Martin, "The Story of "Bloody Jack" Krafchenko" (1998) 35 *Manitoba History* 15.

45.  James McGrath

(a)  *Brandon Sun,* 3 June 1931.

(b)  *Brandon Sun,* 4 June 1931.

(c)  *Brandon Sun,* 9 June 1931.

(d)  *Brandon Sun,* 26 October 1931, p. 1.

(e)  *Brandon Sun,* 17 November 1931, p. 1.

(f)  *Brandon Sun,* 18 November 1931, p.1.

(g)  *Brandon Sun,* 19 November 1931, p. 1.

(h)  *Brandon Sun,* 20 November 1931, p. 1.

(i)  *Brandon Sun,* 2 February 1932, p. 1.

(j)  *Manitoba Free Press,* Wednesday 3 June 1931, p. 1.

(k)  *Manitoba Free Press,* Thursday 4 June 1931, p. 1.

(l)  *Manitoba Free Press,* Thursday 19 November 1931, p. 18.

(m)  *Manitoba Free Press,* Friday 20 November 1931, p. 3.

(n)  *Manitoba Free Press,* 1 February 1932, p. 1.

(o)  *Manitoba Free Press,* 2 February 1932, p. 5.

(p)  "McGrath, James" in Persons Sentenced to Death in Canada, 1876-1976: An Inventory of Case Files in the Fonds of the Department of Justice 211 at data2.archives.ca/pdf/pdf001/p000001052.pdf

(q)  "Mrs. James McGrath", Official Registration of Death, Province of Manitoba, 5 June 1931.

(r)  R.v. McGrath (1932), [1932] 1 W.W.R. 385, 40 Man. R. 139 (C.A.).

46.  Walter Gordon

(a)  Archival material, *Boissevain Recorder.*

(b)  *Boissevain Recorder,* 7 October 1900.

(c)  *Boissevain Recorder,* 11 October 1900.

(d)  *Boissevain Recorder,* 23 January 1902.

(e)  *Boissevain Recorder,* 6 February 1902.

(f)  *Boissevain Recorder,* 11 February 1902.

(g)  *Boissevain Recorder,* 13 February 1902.

(h)  *Boissevain Recorder* 19 June 1902.

(i)  *Boissevain Recorder,* 26 June 1902.

(j)  "Gordon, Walter" in Persons Sentenced to Death in Canada, 1876-1976: An Inventory of Case Files in the Fonds of the Department of Justice, 138 at data2.archhives.ca/pdf/pdf001/p000001052/pdf

47.  William Hickin Webb

(a)  *Brandon Sun,* Thursday 6 September 1888, p. 1.

(b)  *Brandon Sun,* Thursday 22 November 1888, p. 1.

(c)  *Brandon Sun,* Wednesday 26 December 1888, p. 1.

(d)  *Brandon Sun,* Wednesday 2 January 1889, p. 1, 2.

(e)  "Webb, William Hickin" in Persons Sentenced to Death in Canada 1876-1976: An Inventory of Case Files in the Fonds of the Department of Justice, 316 at data2.archives.ca/pdf/pdf001/p000001052.pdf

48.  Lawrence Gowland

(a)  *Brandon Weekly Sun,* 1 June 1907.

(b)  *Brandon Weekly Sun,* Thursday 19 December 1907, p. 2.

(c)  "Gowland, Lawrence" in *Persons Sentenced to Death in Canada, 1876-1976: An Inventory of Case Files in the Fonds of the Department of Justice,* 139 at data2.archives.ca/pdf/pdf001/p000001052.pdf

(d)  *Manitoba Free Press,* Thursday 23 May 1907, p. 1.

(e)  *Manitoba Free Press,* Friday 24 May 1907, p. 1.

(f)  *Manitoba Free Press,* Monday 27 May 1907, p. 7.

(g)  *Manitoba Free Press,* Wednesday 29 May 1907, p. 5.

(h)  *Manitoba Free Press,* Thursday 30 May 1907, p. 1.

(i)  *Manitoba Free Press,* Tuesday 4 June 1907, p. 1.

(j)  *Manitoba Free Press,* Wednesday 23 October 1907, p. 1.

(k)  *Manitoba Free Press,* Thursday 24 October 1907, p. 1.

(l)  *Manitoba Free Press,* Wednesday 11 December 1907, p. 3.

(m)  *Manitoba Free Press,* Thursday 12 December 1907, p. 1.

(n)  *Manitoba Free Press,* Friday 13 December 1907, p. 1.

(o)  *Manitoba Free Press,* Saturday 14 December 1907, p. 19.

49.  Earle 'the Strangler' Nelson

(a)  Burchill, John, "The Strangler" in *Winnipeg Police Service, History & Museum,* Historical Stories at www.winnipeg.ca/police/History/story21.stm

(b)  Garland, Aileen, "Morgan" in *Trails and Crossroads to Killarney* (Killarney: Killarney & District Historical Committee, 1967) 349.

(c)  *Manitoba Free Press,* Saturday 7 January 1928, p. 1.

(d)  *Manitoba Free Press,* Saturday 14 January 1928, p. 4.

(e)  Miller, Orlo, "The Necrophiliac" in *Twenty Mortal Murders: Bizarre Murder Cases From Canada's Past* (Toronto: Macmillan, 1978) 183.

(f) "Nelson, Earle (alias Wilson, Virgil; The Black Strangler)" in
Persons Sentenced to Death in Canada, 1876-1976: An Inventory
of Case Files in the Fonds of the Department of Justice, 231 at
data2.archives.ca/pdf/pdf001/p000001052.pdf

(g) "The Dark Strangler" in *Slabtown Chronicle,* Saturday 22
April 2006 at www.portlandcrime.blogspot.com/2006/04/
dark-strangler.html

50. Manitoba's Only Triple Hanging

(a) "Kanuka, William" in Persons Sentenced to Death in Canada,
1876-1976: An Inventory of Case Files in the Fonds of the
Department of Justice, 167 at data2.archives.ca/pdf/pdf001/
p000001052.pdf

(b) "Korzenowski, Peter", *ibid.,* at 174.

(c) "Prytula, Dan"", *ibid.,* at 254-5.

(d) *Winnipeg Free Press,* Saturday 14 May 1938, p. 1.

(e) *Winnipeg Free Press,* Monday 16 May 1938, p. 1.

(f) *Winnipeg Free Press,* Tuesday 17 May 1938, p. 1.

(g) *Winnipeg Free Press,* Wednesday 18 May 1938, p. 1.

(h) *Winnipeg Free Press,* Thursday 19 May 1938, p. 3.

(i) *Winnipeg Free Press,* Friday 20 May 1938, p. 4.

(j) *Winnipeg Free Press,* Saturday 21 May 1938, p. 2.

(k) *Winnipeg Free Press,* Saturday 28 May 1938, p. 1.

(l) *Winnipeg Free Press,* Wednesday 1 June 1938, p. 1.

(m) *Winnipeg Free Press,* Thursday 2 June 1938, p. 9.

(n) *Winnipeg Free Press,* Wednesday 16 November 1938, p. 1.

(o) *Winnipeg Free Press,* Thursday 17 November 1938, p. 1.

(p) *Winnipeg Free Press,* Friday 18 November 1938, p. 4.

(q) *Winnipeg Free Press,* Tuesday 22 November 1938, p. 1.

(r) *Winnipeg Free Press,* Wednesday 23 November 1938, p. 1.

(s) *Winnipeg Free Press,* Thursday 24 November 1938, p. 1.

(t) *Winnipeg Free Press,* Wednesday 15 February 1938, p. 1.

(u) *Winnipeg Free Press,* Thursday 16 February 1938, p. 1.

# index